THE 12 ESSENTIALS OF GODLY SUCCESS

BEST-SELLING AUTHOR AND SPEAKER

TOMMY NELSON

THE **12**

ESSENTIALS OF

GODLY

SUCCESS

BIBLICAL STEPS *to a* LIFE WELL LIVED

BROADMAN
&HOLMAN
PUBLISHERS

NASHVILLE, TENNESSEE

13-digit ISBN: 978-0-8054-4071-3
10-digit ISBN: 0-8054-4071-2

Published by Broadman & Holman Publishers,
Nashville, Tennessee

Dewey Decimal Classification: 158
Subject Headings: SUCCESS \ CHRISTIAN LIFE

Unless otherwise noted, Scripture quotations have been taken from the
New American Standard Bible, copyright © 1960, 1962, 1963, 1968,
1971, 1972, 1973, 1975, 1977, 1995 by the Lockman Foundation.

1 2 3 4 5 6 7 8 9 10 09 08 07 06 05

Contents

In memory of Ben Newman, my father-in-law.
A husband, father, friend, businessman, soldier, patriot,
leader, grandfather, deacon, philosopher, student, teacher,
and pillar of his day—who lived with excellence the faith
of the Savior he loved and served. Though now with the Lord,
his footsteps live before me still—a true success.

The Biblical Perspective on Success

Everyone wants to succeed. I've never met a single person who wanted to fail and ruin his or her life.

So why do so many people fail in ways that leave them riddled with guilt and regret? Because they never understood the nature of biblical success.

The Bible actually speaks a lot about success. Biblical success is something that you are, not something you merely attain. I wrote this book from my heart as a pastor to help you understand the key ingredients of true success. I'll share with you practical insights about values, integrity, self-control, authority, struggles, peers, a standard of work, and marriage.

Over and over in my ministry, I see folks who get off track in these areas and make a mess of their lives. These are essential areas that we will either master or be mastered by.

Each chapter will help you reflect on your life in light of biblical teaching and make needed changes based on what you learn. This book is not about only learning new information; it's about helping you implement new habits that will shape your life and destiny.

I pray God would use this work to lead you to the success your heart has always longed for.

Acknowledgments

To David Delk and his excellence in assisting the writing of this book.

To Doug Hudson and his diligent actions in bringing dreams to fruition.

To the faithful saints of Denton Bible Church who are my constant joy and who first heard this material.

CHAPTER 1

Foundations:

Success Starts Here

I have always wanted to write a book on success but never have. I've thought and prayed about it, but it never seemed to be the right time. One reason is that it seems everyone else is talking about success. Bookstores are filled with books on success (Amazon.com offers 12,347 tomes on that topic). The Internet is overflowing with information about it (a recent Google search for the word *success* retrieved 37,200,000 Web pages—more than thirty-seven million Web pages that talk about success!). Our man-centered culture is consumed with it.

And yet most of what I have read about success in recent days is just plain wrong. These folks may mean well, but they are misleading people and corrupting the idea of biblical success. If you turn on the TV or read one of these books, you will often find that they are extolling the virtues of the very things the Bible warns about.

Many people today—even Christians—think about success in terms of money. The world is constantly shoving its definition of success down our throats; success is grandeur, greatness, and prosperity.

Yet the Bible is not silent on the subject of success. It's not as if we have to go looking for information or make up a definition of success on our own. The Bible clearly speaks about what makes up a good life and a bad life. The term *success* is used in both the Old and New Testaments. God wants you to be successful. "You will make your way prosperous, and then you will have success" (Josh. 1:8).

But biblical success is much more than just prosperity. Paul said, "I have learned the secret of being filled and going hungry, both of having abundance and suffering need" (Phil. 4:12).

Success is not wealth. Sorry. Success is not having a happy life. People may wish that were true, but it's not. Success is not having all your childhood dreams come true. Success is not having the perfect family. Success is not having everyone like you, think you are attractive, or be amazed at your talent or competence.

If you want to learn about biblical success, the first step is to put to death the worldly view of success that has seeped into your soul. Right now, as you begin this book, ask God to help you wipe the slate clean. Pray and ask Him to give you new eyes to see what success really is. Take that sorry view of success you've absorbed from the world out of your pocket, throw it on the ground, and stomp on it. Then you'll be ready to hear from God and His Word.

Biblical Success

What is biblical success? It is the science of living blessedly. It's the art of living life within God's favor and underneath His gaze.

I felt compelled to write this book because I have spent the last twenty-five years working with Christians who are obviously educated, gifted, orthodox, evangelical, and fundamental, yet they make a mess out of their lives. They harvest tragedy, pain, alienation, loneliness, and in some cases, premature death. They harm their mates and their kids and their families. Some of them end up as lonely, miserable eighty-year-olds with empty, tragic lives. Instead of being like Abraham, they are like his nephew Lot—everything they have goes up in smoke and tragedy. It all happens because they don't know the biblical art of being successful.

Most people are not living biblically successful lives. We are living anemic, mediocre, suburban, American, Christian lives, but we are not living biblically successful lives. Where is the spiritual power that changes the people around us? Where is the deep, soul-satisfying joy that wells up in deep belly laughs at the hilarity of life? Where is steady gladness in God that tempers suffering and allows us to testify to Him even in the midst of tragedy? We know so little of these things because we have settled for something so much less than biblical success.

Success is something you learn. Since the Fall, success hasn't come naturally. We learn it from God through the Bible.

What does the Bible say about the science, the art, the skill of living blessedly? How can you keep from being a clumsy Christian? If I asked you questions about what it means to be a Christian, you might answer them perfectly. You are confident of a time in your life when you accepted Christ as your Savior. And yet your life is not abundant. You are living a life of great pain but not because of some deep, mysterious reason; it is simply an inability on your part to be wise. What kind of person do you have to be to be successful? That's what this book is all about.

Begin with the Fear of God

The place to begin is not with something you do but something you assume—that "the fear of the Lord is the beginning of wisdom" (Prov. 9:10).

What is the fear of God? Recognizing that life is designed by Someone other than me. The fear of God is the recognition that I have been born in alien territory and that the rules for happiness and tragedy are already established. You and I don't get to vote on them. We can choose to deny them, but God is not going to change them based on our suggestions. The fear of God is the recognition that God is the designer of life and that any life lived at odds with His absolute decree is a life that is going to suffer and hurt.

When I was in Russia doing evangelism, a woman named Galena traveled with me. I didn't know the currency of Russia, the rules of Russia, or the language of Russia, but she did. When we traveled, I would not let this woman get one foot away from me. I was her shadow. Do you know why? Because I was afraid and I walked in the fear of losing Galena. I didn't think, act, or choose for myself because I didn't know the lay of the land. She did. She was my life, my mind, my voice, my example. I understood that every foot of distance I allowed to come between this woman and me increased the chances that my life would become perilous and tragic. I also knew that to the degree that I emulated her I would be successful in Russia.

That's the attitude and awareness you should have as a Christian. As King David realized in the Old Testament, "I am a stranger with You" (Ps. 39:12). He admitted, "I'm an alien. I can't make it in this life. Even though I'm in my home country, I don't have a clue. I need You!"

Moses and Success

Leaving Mount Sinai, Moses said, "If Your presence does not go with us, do not lead us up from here. For how then can it be known that I have found favor in Your sight, I and Your people? Is it not by Your going with us, so that we, I and Your people, may be distinguished from all the other people who are upon the face of the earth?" (Exod. 33:15–16).

"God, if You don't go with me, then I will not go from here." Moses was a talented man. He had the best education Egypt could provide. He had the horse sense that came from tending flocks for forty years in the wilderness. He had just accomplished the greatest success of his life in leading the Israelites out of Egypt, where they had been cruelly oppressed by Pharaoh.

And yet Moses said, "I'm not going to make one move unless You're right here with me."

Here is the foundation of success: being so desperately dependent on the presence of God that your life is shaped by your need for Him. Are you convinced of this?

If you don't read your Bible, I'd like to suggest in all the love of Christ that you're really not convinced of this. If you don't know your Bible, it's because you assume a confidence in yourself. And that's a confidence that is not warranted. If you truly recognize the person and position of God, you won't move one step in life in self-confidence. You will know that without the active presence of God in your life, you will end up in a heap of trouble.

I can't tell you how often I hear Christians mock atheists, secularists, and agnostics, and yet these same Christians will live in ignorance, passive indifference, and active rebellion against God. While they are mocking others, they are living as practical atheists with no knowledge of God and no true fear of God. And if "the fear of the Lord is the beginning of wisdom," how much insight do they truly have?

The good news is if you have a strange confidence in yourself and a lack of humility toward God, God can change you in about fifteen seconds. He really can, just by giving you a tablespoon of reality, if He is so pleased. Trust me: a tablespoon is plenty.

I have a friend who is one of the best football coaches in Texas. By his own admission, he struggled with pride until he had a sudden heart attack while working in his garden. In that instant he saw clearly just how vulnerable, weak, and dependent he really was. In his words, "The Bible went from a book and a discipline to my very life." It only takes a moment for God to teach us to cling.

Acquiring Wisdom: Knowing Your Bible

Once you have the fear of God, you can come to the next step: believing that there is a revelation by which you can know God and know yourself. God revealed Himself so that you can understand Him and His creation, including the institutions of family, society, government, work, and people. In other words, you have to gain knowledge and skill about life. "The beginning of wisdom is: Acquire wisdom" (Prov. 4:7).

So, after the fear of God, the next step is the acquisition of wisdom. I have to make a deliberate act to acquire something that I don't have. *Chokmah* is the Hebrew word for "wisdom, skill, or art." It's used in the book of Exodus for the designing of the tabernacle. The artisans who sewed the tabernacle materials did so with chokmah—great skill. In the book of Isaiah, war is waged with chokmah—there meaning the ability to win.

And in the book of Ezekiel, chokmah is used about becoming wealthy, describing the ability to turn a nickel into a quarter.

That's what the Old Testament describes as wisdom—the ability to be artistic, victorious, and prosperous. It's the art of life. It's the skill of living. It's learning to play by the rules of the game. Proverbs 8 exhorts us to acquire wisdom because wisdom is woven into the very order of creation. It is the foundation of reality.

How do you become wise? You go to the Bible.

Paul said, "If any man among you thinks that he is wise in this age, he must become foolish, so that he may become wise" (1 Cor. 3:18). Wisdom is born out of humility and the recognition of our own ignorance. That's what leads us to come to God for help.

We had a term for this in the old days—"savvy." You probably don't hear that too much anymore. It came from *saber* (to know) in Spanish and *savoir* (to know) in French, both of which came from the Latin *sapere*.

Now that's what God has to be to you—the One who helps you to have "savvy" in life.

In 1 Kings, we read the story of the beginning of Solomon's reign in Israel. God appears to him in a dream and says, "What would you like?"

Solomon replies, "I am but a little child; I do not know how to go out or come in . . . give Your servant an understanding heart to judge Your people" (1 Kings 3:7, 9).

To God, that was a delightful prayer. He was so pleased that a man would humbly admit his ignorance. To paraphrase, Solomon said, "God, I'm an idiot." He was at least twenty years old at the time but confessed, "I am but a child." He essentially said, "I can't make it unless You show me how to pull this stuff off."

The beginning of wisdom, Solomon said, is the recognition that you need wisdom. A lot of Americans—specifically, a lot of American males—are not wise because they think they are smart. Esteeming your own intelligence is totally useless from the perspective of the Bible: "If any man among you thinks that he is wise in this age, he must become foolish, so that he may become wise" (1 Cor. 3:18).

God knows the reasoning of smart people is often unhelpful. Being smart merely means you have the ability to acquire knowledge quickly. If smart means you learn quickly, wisdom means that you forget slowly. Wisdom can integrate knowledge. The ability to earn degrees and solve brainteasers with your high IQ has absolutely nothing to do with happiness. As a matter of fact, faith in your intelligence often can be an impediment to happiness. All kinds of smart people have wrecked their lives and just assumed they're not to blame, simply because they've got a couple of university degrees. Wisdom is not that you *can* learn but *what* you learn.

The Bible doesn't care if you're smart—that doesn't mean anything. But you do have to be wise.

If you are on a ship that springs a leak, the crew will immediately seal off the leaky area to keep it from affecting the rest of the ship. That's what we smart people have done with God: we have sealed Him off. We make God and religion separate from everyday life. We separate philosophy from life. Too many Christians make church and biblical knowledge separate from life. But if we want true success, we simply cannot do that. "The Lord knows the reasonings of the wise, that they are useless" (1 Cor. 3:20).

Wisdom is not just orthodoxy; wisdom is applying God's truth to the reality of life. Wisdom is the ability to learn from God. Wisdom is birthed from the humility that recognizes the two undeniable truths of life; one, there is a God, and two, I am not He. Once you have this recognition, wisdom is the discipline to come to the Bible and learn from God.

The goal of this book is to help you understand success—the biblical success that comes from true wisdom lived out by real people in everyday life. If you'll fear God and go to His Word, you can taste success that will satisfy your soul.

So join me for a journey as we turn the world's definition of success upside down and replace it with eternal truth from God's holy Word. It just might change your life.

Biblical success comes when you

1. understand that God wants you to find true success (Josh. 1:8),
2. learn to live under the blessing and favor of God,
3. walk in fear and reverence for God,
4. become desperately dependent on the presence of God,
5. acquire wisdom by studying and devouring the Word of God.

A PRAYER FOR TRUE SUCCESS

Father, though our hearts wander and are distracted by many things, we want to revere and fear You. Will You give us the grace to think rightly about who You are and what You have done? Help us to love Your Word and to absorb its truth. Help us to depend on You for every moment and every breath, knowing that it is only in You we can find true success. We ask this in Jesus' name. Amen.

THINKING MORE DEEPLY ABOUT TRUE SUCCESS

1. What do you think are some of the dominant definitions of success prevalent in our culture today? Which ones have had the most impact on you? Why?

2. What are some of the consequences for people who adopt a wrong view of success? How have you seen this in your own life or the lives of others?

3. What does it mean to "fear God"? What does this look like in your life? How can you increase the "fear of God" to help you stay on the path to success?

4. What would it mean for you to be "desperately dependent" on the presence of God? How would this change your life?

5. How consistently do you study God's Word? Why or why not? How has your life been shaped by God's truth, and what changes might come if you acquired more wisdom from the Bible?

CHAPTER 2

Relationships:

The Ability to Work and Play Well with Others

When I was in seminary, a gentleman named Bob worked for the school's placement office, helping seminary graduates find employment in churches. On one occasion a friend named Mel was in his office and noticed a large stack of papers on Bob's desk. Mel asked, "Bob, whose résumés are those?"

"Those are the men graduating from our seminary that we cannot place in churches," Bob said.

"What makes them hard to place?" Mel pursued.

"Because they can't get along with humans," Bob replied. "They are marvelous with theology, they are great debaters, but nobody likes them. They're arrogant and rude and inflexible."

Wisdom is not truly wisdom unless it is lived out in the context of relationships. We are made in the image of a God who is the Trinity. As the Trinity, God exists in relationships—Father, Son, and Holy Spirit. He's personal. He made us to be personal.

The idea of a loner is unbiblical. A hermit is unbiblical. A convent is unbiblical. A monastery is unbiblical. You have to integrate with other humans—to love, to be sensitive, to be kind, giving, and caring—like your heavenly Father. You can't be happy away from people. You can't be holy away from people. You can't be wise away from people. And you can't be significant away from people. "He who separates himself seeks his own desire" (Prov. 18:1).

Sometimes we don't like that. We like to escape. Even when we're in a crowd, we wear a mask to make sure nobody gets inside. But such actions distort the image of God in us, taking away wisdom and thwarting success.

Jesus was asked, "What is the greatest commandment?" He said it was to love God and your neighbor. Saying that you love God while being an unkind, unloving human being is totally contradictory. After more than thirty years of pastoring, I've seen a bunch of folks who don't find success because they can't get along with people. Let me give you, from my experience and from God's Word, the top forty ways to ensure failure in relationships.

Forty Ways to Guarantee Failure with People

When I first preached on the topic of success, Jim Hill, the church's administrator, asked me, "How are you going to end your message?"

I said, "I'm going to give forty reasons why people won't like you."

He said, "Me, personally?"

In this chapter I am going to ask you forty questions that show not why people won't like Jim Hill but you. If you're a person who is a sociological disaster, if you are sad and lonely, it's usually because of choices you have made. Your life is like a briar patch to everyone who comes near you. If any of these forty characteristics dominate your life, you are guaranteed to never find biblical success.

These are not sophisticated, Ph.D. philosophies from academia; these are forty common-sense tidbits you'll pick up in Sunday school and from God's Word. Some of these will hit home with you. Feel free to initial others for the person you will pass this book to.

When I taught this list at my church, it was fascinating to see the crowd reactions—wives elbowing husbands, daughters nudging their moms, brothers snickering at something their dad did. You may not have anyone sitting beside you right now to give you an elbow in the ribs, but why not let the Holy Spirit do that in your heart?

Without further ado, here are the top forty relational questions that will determine whether you will be a failure in your life.

1. Are you a loner?

Back to Proverbs 18:1—"He who separates himself seeks his own desire."

The reason people run from personal connections is not because they are godly, but because they don't want anybody making demands on their own selfish lifestyles. Jesus was called the friend of sinners. Are you withdrawn? You need to work on it. You can't spend all your time with God and none with men. You can't always be with men and never with God. The reason you're with God is so that you can go among men. Samson had friends only among the Philistines—not the best accountability group. Who keeps you on track?

2. Are you a bad listener?

Nobody likes being interrupted or being responded to in a way that shows their listener doesn't care about what they are saying. Proverbs 18:13 says, "He who gives an answer before he hears, it is folly and shame to him."

Don't you just love it when you're explaining your heart to someone and they interrupt you? A man once said to me, "I do something I think my wife may not like."

"What is it?" I asked.

He said, "As she starts telling me how she feels, I say, 'Uh-huh, uh-huh.'"

"Yeah, I think you're on to something," I said.

People don't like to be interrupted. Learn to be a good listener.

3. Do you give your opinion before people ask?

Proverbs 12:23 says, "A prudent man conceals knowledge, but the heart of fools proclaims folly."

Don't you love to be around know-it-alls? When you're around a know-it-all, don't you just want to stop and say, "How did you become so brilliant?" Sometimes you're tempted to say, "Would you please shut up, you obnoxious person?"

A wise man, on the other hand, conceals knowledge. A wise man makes you draw what he knows out of him. He's not always volunteering his brilliance.

4. Are you argumentative?

"Blessed are the peacemakers, for they shall be called sons of God" (Matt. 5:9).

Remember that the mark of the sons of God is to be "peacemakers." No one admires the argumentative for his oratorical skills, but all love the peacemaker.

5. Are you unforgiving?

Proverbs 20:3 says, "Keeping away from strife is an honor for a man, but any fool will quarrel."

Are you one of these people who has rigid moral standards (which is good), but when someone violates them, you open up on them with verbal napalm (which is bad). If you take pride in knowing that people will only cross you once, you will never have true success.

6. Do you say things to cut someone off at the knees?

Proverbs 12:18 says, "There is one who speaks rashly like the thrusts of a sword, but the tongue of the wise brings healing."

Nobody likes to be around a verbal bully who humiliates or dominates other people.

7. Do you explode when you get mad?

Another great proverb for the home is Proverbs 18:19—"A brother offended is harder to be won than a strong city, and contentions are like the bars of a citadel."

If you explode at someone, you can't absolve it by saying, "Well, I'm awful sorry. Can we forget about it and go on?" You can't do that in life. When you go off on your mate or your kid, you're pulling a pin on a grenade. The shrapnel flies out and causes scar tissue. You may walk away and forget about it, but they can't.

Need to test this point? Go out in your backyard and kick your dog in the head real hard four or five times and then whistle and see if he'll come. (I'm just kidding—but you get the point.)

I counsel husbands who say, "My wife won't open up to me anymore." I have to tell many of them that she won't because she doesn't trust them. You've smoked her so many times that she can't trust you anymore. You can't explode and find success.

8. Are you too blunt?

Proverbs 29:11 says, "A fool always loses his temper."

Do you know people who pride themselves on being "honest" and "truthful"? Get away from them as fast as you can! No verses in the Bible admonish you to express all your thoughts. In fact, the Bible consistently tells us to control our speech, not to express everything.

Let me make this point in a way that you will never forget. What are the last muscles that infants develop control over? Sphincters—the ones that keep you from spitting up or accidentally having a bowel movement. If we never developed that control, we would embarrass ourselves every day.

I've met a lot of people who need a verbal sphincter in their lives. They have never developed the moral sense to not say the vile things that are down in their throats. They may as well be a baby filling their diapers.

9. Do you drop the ball when people are relying on you?

Proverbs 10:26 says, "Like vinegar to the teeth and smoke to the eyes, so is the lazy one to those who send him."

Don't you just love those people who don't follow through when you're relying on them? They make you grit your teeth!

Don't be irresponsible. If you are, people will keep their distance. Do what you've agreed to and draw folks to you.

10. Are you a selfish person?

Proverbs 11:26 says, "He who withholds grain, the people will curse him, but blessing will be on the head of him who sells it."

Some of the greatest villains in literature have been selfish men. Silas Marner and Ebenezer Scrooge thought they were wise and frugal. They were actually stingy and selfish and hated by all. The Bible never commands us to hoard. God gives you money to sow and be a blessing to others. Learn to give liberally.

11. Do you make fun of other people?

Proverbs 17:5 says, "He who rejoices at calamity will not go unpunished."

God hates people making sport of the pain of others because God doesn't make sport of us; He heals us. All children seem to go through this stage of poking fun at someone else to make themselves look good. Eventually it's time to grow up. Find your security in Christ and leave other people alone.

12. Are you two-faced?

Proverbs 10:6 says, "The mouth of the wicked conceals violence."

Wicked people smile to your face but nail you behind your back. The Old Testament calls this person a backbiter. The problem with stabbing someone in the back is that eventually they turn around and then you have to deal with them face-to-face. You will never find biblical success if you are two-faced.

13. Can you not keep a secret?

Proverbs 11:13 says, "He who goes about as a talebearer reveals secrets."

Have you shared a private issue only to find out later that the person you told it to spread your news to others? That causes you to lose a lot of trust, doesn't it?

That's why the Old Testament says, "Don't associate with a gossip." In the New Testament, Paul said people were going "around from house to house . . . talking about things not proper to mention" and that "some have already turned aside to follow Satan" (1 Tim. 5:13, 15). You are following in the footsteps of Satan when you gossip because Satan by his nature is an accuser of the brethren.

Do you know why we love to gossip? Because we immediately take center stage when we share news about others. We can make ourselves look good and someone else look bad.

Be trustworthy with intimate knowledge and keep it to yourself.

14. Are you an inflexible, controlling perfectionist?

Proverbs 14:4 says, "Where no oxen are, the manger is clean, but much revenue comes by the strength of the ox."

To get work done, you have to have oxen. And if you have oxen, you will have a mess. You can keep your barn perfect, but you won't get any work done.

Are you so controlling and inflexible about the messes of life that nobody can put up with you? Sometimes this vice is even labeled as a virtue, but there's nothing virtuous about such demanding, ungraceful behavior. I counseled a husband once who justified his anger at his wife because she failed to pick up four magnolia leaves on the front lawn. You probably don't want to know what I said to that man.

The point is that we can't always have life the way we want it. In a fallen world, you have to flex to find biblical success.

15. Are you an insensitive person?

Proverbs 27:14 says, "He who blesses his friend with a loud voice early in the morning, it will be reckoned a curse to him."

My wife might underline this section for me. This proverb shows that even though you said good words, you were insensitive as to when and how and where you said them.

We are personal beings made in the image of God. We're the only animal who can take thoughts and emotions and, with the contraction of the diaphragm, push air up over our larynx and vocal cords to create a column of sound. Then you can take your tongue and hard and soft palettes and shape that sound into words. You can cut those words up wherever you want and put them into another person's mind and soul. You can make people feel anyway you want to. Think about it—"aiee luv yuu" or "drop ded." You can manipulate other people by what you say.

Isn't that terrible that God made us with such power? You can never find success if you are insensitive to the souls of others.

16. Are you unsympathetic or unfeeling?

Proverbs 25:20 says, "Like one who takes off a garment on a cold day, or like vinegar on soda, is he who sings songs to a troubled heart."

When someone is hurting and you are singing, it just makes them wither. When somebody's hurting, weep with those who weep. Can you feel the same pain that somebody else feels?

17. Do you use other people?

Proverbs 23:1–3 says that when you are eating with a rich man you should put a knife to your throat because his morsels are deceptive.

What does that mean? Proverbs often use rich people as a foil—not because all rich people are evil but because many rich people get that way through compromise and sin. If you have strip clubs in your city, find out where the owner lives. I guarantee you he's doing well in this world.

The idea of this verse is that you better be careful when you eat with a man like this because although he looks nice he isn't—he's manipulative. Are you a manipulative person? Do you use people for your own ends? If so, you will never find success.

18. Do you have uncontrolled anger?

Proverbs 19:19 says, "A man of great anger will bear the penalty, for if you rescue him, you will only have to do it again."

If you help an angry person out of trouble, he'll eventually land there again. Letting your anger run wild can be addictive.

Unfettered anger goes off like a hand grenade, throwing out shrapnel and destroying everyone around. Deal with the source of your anger or you will never find success.

19. Are you rude?

Proverbs 18:23 says, "The rich man answers roughly."

No person has attained to such a place as to be inconsiderate to others.

Proverbs 25:11 says, "Like apples of gold in settings of silver is a word spoken in right circumstances."

Success comes when we are careful to say the right word in the right way at the right time. One who is sensitive to others with his words is as beautiful in his discourse as gold and silver.

20. Do you have a critical spirit?

Proverbs 16:21 says that "sweetness of speech increases persuasiveness."

If all you do is tell people what they are doing wrong, they eventually won't want to talk to you anymore.

21. Are you a mooch?

Proverbs 30:15 says, "The leech has two daughters, 'Give,' 'Give.'"

Don't you just love someone who is always taking? If people see you as someone who always wants something from them, you'll never find success.

22. Are you a liar?

Proverbs 19:5 says, "A false witness will not go unpunished, and he who tells lies will not escape."

Are you a liar or do you just speak "evangelasticly," where you stretch truth to make it fit the subject? None of us wants to admit that we don't tell the truth, but are you scrupulously honest? It's so easy to say things in a way that paints us in the best possible light. But if you want to find success, you have to be honest. In your honesty don't forget to be sensitive but "speak truth each one of you with his neighbor" (Eph. 4:25).

23. Are you sarcastic?

Proverbs 14:9 says, "Fools mock at sin, but among the upright there is good will."

A wicked person thinks evil is a funny thing. Our world today takes things that are profane and makes them the objects of jokes. When offensive ideas or actions become a source of humor, they don't seem so offensive anymore.

24. Do you have trouble admitting you're wrong?

Proverbs 14:8 says, "The wisdom of the sensible is to understand his way, but the foolishness of fools is deceit."

Whenever I counsel someone new, I begin by asking them a question: Are you wise or are you foolish? They usually reply, "What's the difference?" and I quote this verse.

If you're not going to admit you have needs, I can't help you. You may as well go home and keep making a disaster of your life. If you won't admit up front that you are wrong and start appropriating the wisdom of others, you are choosing to get beaten up by life.

25. Are you a pessimist?

Proverbs 15:15 says, "All the days of the afflicted are bad, but a cheerful heart has a continual feast."

Don't you just love "Eeyore" kind of people? Remember Winnie the Pooh's donkey buddy, Eeyore? "Great day. It'll probably rain." I have a friend in the ministry that I love, though it is a struggle sometimes to be around his wife. She's the kind of woman who at the throne of glory will gripe about the glare.

If you are constantly looking at the bad side of your circumstances, you will never find success.

26. Are you inconsiderate?

Paul admonishes us to look out not only for our own interests but also the interests of others (Phil. 2:4). With the hectic pace of life, it's easy to focus so much on ourselves that we forget the people around us. If you are too focused on yourself, you will never find success.

27. Are you self-centered?

Proverbs 25:27 says, "It is not good to eat much honey, nor is it glory to search out one's own glory."

Nobody likes a self-centered person who longs to declare their own praises. Too much of anyone is sickening. If you view the world solely from the perspective of how things affect you, watch out—you will never find success.

28. Are you overly sensitive?

Proverbs 12:16 says, "A fool's anger is known at once, but a prudent man conceals dishonor."

A fool immediately goes off in anger, but a wise person can take a hit and know how to deal with it. They absorb it, pray it through, then express themselves wisely.

29. Are you codependent?

Proverbs 25:16–17 says, "Have you found honey? Eat only what you need, that you not have it in excess and vomit it. Let your foot rarely be in your neighbor's house, or he will become weary of you and hate you."

Too much of a good thing is bad. Have you ever had a friend you were afraid to be nice to because you knew they would be like an old dog that you have to take home for the rest of your life?

Benjamin Franklin said, "Fish and visitors stink in three days."

When I talk to our singles about dating, I really hammer this home. A young man takes a girl out; likes her; by the end of the evening, says he loves her; and by the time he drops her off at home, he's naming the kids. His emotions are running so fast ahead of him that he just overwhelms her and violates her emotionally. I tell these young men, "Don't let this happen. Don't be waiting there the next morning when she gets up to get the paper." She'll think she's dating Norman Bates.

Have your deepest needs met in Christ, so you don't have to ask people to do more for you than they can do.

30. Are you jealous?

Proverbs 27:4 says, "Wrath is fierce and anger is a flood, but who can stand before jealousy?"

No one likes to be around a jealous person.

31. Do you run hot and cold in relationships?

Proverbs 17:17 says, "A friend loves at all times, and a brother is born for adversity."

People want to know that you are going to be committed, that you will be there when they really need you. Be a friend who is a friend when the chips are down. There can be no true friendship without faithfulness.

32. Are you cold?

Proverbs 27:5 says, "Better is open rebuke than love that is concealed."

The opposite of love is not hate—it's apathy. Do you have the ability to show love? If you don't feel connected to the important people in your life, ask God to change your heart. A cold person will never find biblical success.

33. Are you lazy?

Proverbs 20:4 says, "The sluggard does not plow after the autumn, so he begs during the harvest and has nothing."

If you're a lazy person, people won't want to get close to you because they know you will use them.

34. Are you arrogant?

Proverbs 16:18 says, "Pride goes before destruction, and a haughty spirit before stumbling."

If you are arrogant, people may tolerate you because they have to, but they won't really like you. And you will never be able to have biblical success.

35. Do you raise your voice?

Proverbs 15:1 says, "A harsh word stirs up anger."

People don't like yellers. If you grew up in a house where there was yelling, you know how much people want to get away from someone who yells.

36. Do you slander others?

Proverbs 25:23 says, "The north wind brings forth rain, and a backbiting tongue, an angry countenance."

Don't think you can slander people with impunity. You may get away with it for a little while, but eventually it will catch up to you. Slanderous people are always unhappy people.

37. Do you make false promises?

Proverbs 25:14 says, "Like clouds and wind without rain is a man who boasts of his gifts falsely."

Are you someone who writes checks with their mouth that their body can't cash? Don't promise what you can't tender.

38. Do you have a problem with authority?

Proverbs 30:17 says, "The eye that mocks a father and scorns a mother, the ravens of the valley will pick it out, and the young eagles will eat it."

Rebellious people cause trouble wherever they go. Eventually, successful people will get away from you to avoid being collateral damage.

39. Do you always think you are right?

Proverbs 26:16 says, "The sluggard is wiser in his own eyes than seven men who can give a discreet answer."

Nobody likes a know-it-all. Even if you are right most of the time, learn to not rub it in people's faces.

40. Are you pompous?

Proverbs 12:9 says, "Better is he who is lightly esteemed and has a servant than he who honors himself and lacks bread."

In Texas we say, "All hat and no cattle" about these kind of people. Don't be a pompous fraud. Don't esteem yourself more highly than others around you. If people want to give you awards and honors, accept them graciously—just don't give them to yourself.

How did you do? Why don't you spend some time in prayer and ask God to show you four or five of these to work on?

Every area of your life will eventually be affected by the quality of your relationships. If you don't have integrity with people, you can never find biblical success.

Biblical success comes when you

1. recognize that biblical success must be lived out in relationships,
2. honestly evaluate whether you are living out biblical principles,
3. deal with the heart issues that are leading to destructive behaviors with others.

A Prayer for True Success

Father, relationships can be messy. We are sinful and needy people. Help us to come to You first before we manipulate and aggravate the people in our lives. Protect us from ourselves—help us to be instruments of good rather than forces of destruction. May we represent You well as we treat others with dignity and respect, leading them to a closer walk with You. We ask this in Jesus' name. Amen.

Thinking More Deeply about True Success

1. Is it true that you will never find true success unless you learn to get along with people? Why or why not?

2. After reading this list of forty questions, which ones hit home with you? Why did those questions catch your attention?

3. Which of these characteristics do you dislike most in another person? Why do you think that is?

4. If you recognize one of these traits in your life, how can you change? What steps could you take this week that would make a difference in your life?

CHAPTER 3

Values:

What Do You Treasure?

A lfred Nobel is one of the most famous men in history. You
know him because of the Nobel Prize mentions in the news.
His name is still world renowned almost a century after his death.
But you may not know how Mr. Nobel acquired the $8.5 million
he invested in securities in 1901 to fund these prizes in perpetu-
ity. It's a very instructive story.

Alfred Nobel took over his father's business, making mines
and torpedoes for submarines, then began to look for the next
breakthrough product. He devoted himself to research and finally invented what became his chief patent: dynamite. Sales of
dynamite made an already wealthy Alfred Nobel fabulously rich.

You might wonder how someone who built his life on producing military weapons became synonymous for humanitarian
causes today. It happened in a very odd way.

In 1888, one of Alfred Nobel's brothers died, but a French
newspaper mistakenly thought it was Alfred and ran an obituary for him in the next day's edition, calling him the "merchant
of death." Distressed at his legacy of dynamite and destruction, he decided to carve a different place in history. So in

his will he earmarked 94 percent of his net worth—$8.5 million—to be used in awarding prizes for outstanding efforts in humanitarian causes.

Alfred Nobel was able to change his legacy. Like Ebenezer Scrooge, he had the privilege of seeing his end before it came and the opportunity to change. He found out it is possible to fail in life because you have succeeded in all the wrong things. It is possible, as the poet William Watson said, "to house the chaff and to burn the grain."

In life, both good and evil actions often don't have immediate results. So you can live for years and years, looking for human acclaim and immediate gratification, and it can seem like it's working. You can fulfill your physical and lustful desires without any immediate negative results. There may not be any signs that you are headed down a path that leads to emptiness.

Values Are the Foundation

That's why values are the most important thing about you. Values are even more important than intelligence, gifts, abilities, and hard work because you can have all those assets and still succeed at the wrong things. If you aim your gun at the ground, you don't have a chance of hitting a duck. Without the right values, you are predetermined to fail at what really matters.

Whether you esteem the things of God or of earth, the infinite or the finite, the eternal or the temporal, the immediate or the lasting, these values will determine your goals and your ambitions. Your goals and ambitions determine your priorities—how you spend your energy, time, and money. Your priorities will determine your decisions, and your decisions will determine your destiny. It is an unbroken chain that begins with your values. So after you build a foundation of fear in God, you next need to align your values with the heart of God.

First John 2:16–17 says, "For all that is in the world, the lust of the flesh and the lust of the eyes and the boastful pride of life, is not from the Father, but is from the world. The world is passing away, and also its lusts; but the one who does the will of God lives forever." It doesn't make any sense to succeed in an arena that will ultimately pass away.

If I know what you believe about God and this world, then I can predict how you are going to live. If you're consistent with your values, I could ask you a few simple questions and tell whether you will end up empty or full.

Jesus said, "Do not store up for yourselves treasures on earth, where moth and rust destroy, and where thieves break in and steal" (Matt. 6:19).

We all have clothes that wear out and cars that rust. These things are not wrong in themselves, but there's a difference between using them as a means and having them become your purpose in life. Don't make the stuff of this world your treasure and your joy.

Jesus gives us a different thing to covet, a different value system—"Store up for yourselves treasures in heaven, where neither moth nor rust destroys" (Matt. 6:20). These treasures will stand the test of time. Thieves can't break in and steal them; they are absolutely secure.

Why is this choice of values so important? Because "where your treasure is, there your heart will be also" (Matt. 6:21).

Where your values are, your heart will follow. If you treasure the things of this world, then your life and heart are going to follow. Jesus gives us an illustration of this: "The eye is the lamp of the body; so then if your eye is clear, your whole body will be full of light. But if your eye is bad, your whole body will be full of darkness" (Matt. 6:22–23).

Values Are the Eye of the Soul

What does Jesus mean? A lamp guides your body and gives you light. If your lamp is clear, if it doesn't fail you, then your whole body can walk in the light. You will see and not stumble as you walk to the end of the path. Of course, if the lamp goes out or if it falters, you are in trouble. You won't be able to stay on the path.

One of the ways educators are trying to combat the escalating occasions of drunk driving is through the use of goggles that simulate what it is like to be drunk. You can see shapes through these goggles, but they bend and distort the light in different directions, throwing off your equilibrium and approximating the effects of alcohol. The goal is to demonstrate to kids that drinking impairs their ability to make sense of what they see.

Jesus says this world impairs our ability to make sense of what we see. The lamp of your physical body is your eye because your eye illumines your path. It gives us light. So if your vision is clear, then you don't have to worry. Your body will be able to follow the correct path.

Just as in a physical body, your spirit depends upon how it sees. In the area of values, the lamp of your body is how you value things of God or things of the earth. If your eye is clear—if it's not diseased, if you see correctly the things of God and the things of man, the things of heaven and the things of earth, the things that last and the things that don't—then your entire body is well lit. It's going to reach the end for which God designed you and you will find success.

But Jesus says, "If your eye is bad, if your lamp goes out, you're in trouble." If your eye is bad—if it's materialistic, worldly, and hedonistic—then your entire body is going to follow a bad path and you will be hurt. It's like the old saying, "I climbed to the top of my ladder to find it was leaning against the wrong building."

Just as the eye is the most important guide in directing a human body, so values are the most important guide in directing your life. You can succeed in the wrong things and be a failure! When's the last time you met a goal only to find that it left a bitter taste in your mouth?

Money, career, jobs—stuff that the TV and magazines have been telling us about since we were ten—those things can make you a living; they cannot make you a life. Pleasure can invigorate a life and make it temporarily bearable, but pleasure cannot support a life. Only God can do that.

What Is Success?

A man in our church served as the chair of the Department of Finance at the University of North Texas for nine years. He is still a tough professor. He knows finance, how to accrue money, the safe things to do with it, the foolish things to do with it, and how to reproduce it.

I love how he teaches his class. Most of these eighteen-to-twenty-year-olds have already absorbed a new version of the Golden Rule—the one who has the gold makes the rules. And that's become their philosophy of life.

Since they were little, they've been taught to strive for success. The only problem is no one told them what success really was. They learned it had to do with your appearance, your wealth, your house, your car, and all that stuff. So for them, success has to do with physical possessions.

As he lectures on making and managing money, he stops, turns to his class, and says, "Incidentally, make a note here, as you learn all of this stuff; it ultimately doesn't make a hill of beans of difference in your life. If you didn't learn what the kindergarten teacher taught you about being obedient to authority and considerate and kind and loving, you can learn all this stuff and you will be a wealthy waste. Now, let's continue."

Learning how to handle money without values is a waste. A builder ought to say, "I can build you a beautiful five-thousand-square-foot home with rosewood and teakwood, but remember that this house will not automatically be a home." You can have someone build you the prettiest house in the world, and then you can live your disastrous, angry, worthless life in a big luxurious environment. It's a house, not a home; it's a body, not a life. Or as Jesus said, "Life [is] more than food, and the body more than clothing" (Matt. 6:25).

Only God can make a home. We can't find happiness in a house because we are made in the image of God and He's eternal. The same thing is not true of a gerbil; they're not created in the image of God. A life and a living are the same thing to a gerbil. A life and a living are the same to goldfish—the aquarium with a few plants and a little plastic house is fine because they're not created in the image of God. Everything about them is lower story, temporal, and finite; their life consists solely of biological responses.

But because we are made in the image of God, if we try to live only for temporal pleasure we end up hating life. The Bible says God "has also set eternity in [our] heart" (Eccles. 3:11). And we will never ever be satisfied with what makes a goldfish happy.

We're only satisfied by what William Watson called "the things that are more excellent."

Standing against the Tide

I know this is not the message that assails you every day. That's why I am writing this book and belaboring this point a little bit. I know that when you put this book down and watch some TV, you're going to be assaulted by a very different message. When you see billboards as you drive down the road, they are going to beat at your soul. We are constantly bombarded with the idea that fame equals greatness and wealth equals happiness. Everyone wants to treat you like a goldfish that needs one more plastic plant.

A word of caution here: Please remember that, biblically speaking, worldliness has nothing to do with your income. You can't say that wealthy people are worldly. You can't say that poor people are solid in their values. Worldliness or wisdom has nothing to do with your income.

It's how you view your income that matters. Is it something to help you survive in life, to be used for the glory of God? Or is it something you rest on? You have to decide whether you believe your income is your life or not.

Most of us need to be weaned off of this idea that there's this brass ring out there, and if we could have this—if we could make this, if we could possess this, if we could marry this type of trophy woman, if we could just get this type of guy, if we could just get to live here—then we'd have everything we wanted and be happy. The Bible compares this to chasing an elusive bird (Prov. 23:4–5). Every time you get close to him, he flies away. You take a few steps closer and think you are going to catch him, and he flies away again. Even though you think you might catch him at any moment, you never can and you never do.

No man or woman has ever gotten to that square-footage place or that retirement nest egg place or that perfect family place where they could stop and say, "Now I've made it. This is Utopia!" This world is not our home, and we will never find our ideal place in this life. You have to decide if you are going to live like a goldfish or a human being. Remember that the word *utopia* literally means "no place."

We're so hardheaded that most of us don't come to grips with this truth until we chase that bird and taste the emptiness of worldly success, the excess of success, or the price of success. You see, when you say yes to one thing, you have to say no to something else. Often people who define success as wealth have to say no to their family. And often, twenty to thirty years pass before they realize they've said no to the wrong thing.

My Experience with Values

From the time I was a little boy, I had a sense of my mortality and somehow knew life was a phantom. I felt like I had a clock ticking in my head, reminding me I was going to die and my life had to count. I guess you could say I was having a child's version of an existential crisis.

I've never needed an alarm clock my entire life. (My wife says I don't even know how to work one.) I always, even as a little boy, sat straight up in bed at 6:00 a.m. When the cartoons came on, I was there, waiting.

I was so anxious about life that I didn't want to miss a minute of it. I knew somehow wealth wasn't the answer because I had too many buddies that were from well-to-do families and they weren't happy. I'd been in their houses and seen what they were like. So I knew that wasn't it. It only took a year or two of school for me to realize that depending on my native intelligence was not going to be a productive goal for me.

I felt I would be a success if I could make my name live on after I died. The only path that seemed to offer such fame for me was an athletic path, so football and baseball became my activities. I made it all the way to college without discovering that I would not be the greatest quarterback of the century. When the news broke, it was a revelation to me.

Our team was 0 and 3 when it hit me. The coach benched me at halftime during a game against that great eastern power, the University of Akron. I was in school in the 1970s, enjoying the era of Joe Theismann and Archie Manning and Jim Plunkett. I finally had to face the reality that I wouldn't ever be as good as they were.

As I sat on the bench, I felt like I had just been given a terminal diagnosis. Football wasn't just something I enjoyed; football was my life. It gave me meaning, or I hoped it would. It did as long as I won, but I wasn't winning anymore.

During my classes, I began to observe in professors and peers that their lives were like sand castles. Some had big sand castles, some had little sand castles, but I could tell that ultimately the ocean was going to get them. I knew they would be gone and nothing would be left.

About that time I heard the gospel with new ears. The notion that we were eternal beings who could have eternal life reached to the deepest recesses of my soul. I didn't just have to be a recipient of heaven later on; I could be a participant in God's program now. I could spend my life bringing others to the knowledge of this message. I could, by the hammer and chisel of the Bible, help them build a truly successful, soul-satisfying life. That notion was the most wonderful thing I had ever known. I could be a fellow worker with God.

Transcendent Success

Throughout history, great people—not famous ones; there is a big difference—transcend wealth, houses, clothing, and material things. We innately recognize that certain people are committed to more noble things.

Mother Teresa was revered because she was committed to the nobility of the image of God in man. She believed the people of Calcutta are worthy of a noble death, of having someone there to care for them. Father Damien was lauded for voluntarily moving to a leper colony in Hawaii in the late 1800s to serve the lepers, eventually falling to the disease himself.

Ask the average person, and Gandhi would be in their top ten list of great men. Even though most people have no idea what he stood for, they know that he lived for something higher than wealth. He gave up his legal practice and assumed the role of a poor Indian to secure the freedom of native Indians from the British. He called for a hunger strike to bring peace among warring Indians who were Muslims and Hindus. He committed to fast until he died unless his brothers repented.

The idea of living for the freedom of other men is transcendent. Now no matter what you think of Hinduism—and I don't think much of it—there's something attractive about a man who lived for something more than material things and his legal practice.

Abraham Lincoln committed himself to the abolition of slavery and so is remembered as great. Dr. Martin Luther King

Jr., Martin Luther, John Calvin—all are people who committed themselves to ideas bigger than the here and now. Do you know who was recently named the most influential person of the last millennium? Johann Gutenberg, the man who committed his life to helping knowledge be disseminated through the printing press.

You and I have a birthright of greatness. We can commit our lives to those things that will not wash away—to God, His Word, human souls, and eternity. What a privilege, not just to know God forever, but that we can participate in His program. Don't throw this inheritance away for something that will be gone in the blink of an eye. Missionary Jim Elliot said, "The man is no fool who gives up what he cannot keep to gain what he cannot lose."

Haggai and the Return to Jerusalem

We see a great example of people giving up what they have for something greater in the book of Haggai. It's the third to last book of your Old Testament, if you want to read the whole story. (If you haven't read it, I'd encourage you to do so. Otherwise, what will you do in glory when you meet Haggai and he asks, "How'd you like my book?")

Haggai paints a scenario that might sound familiar to some of us. Israel was in the captivity of Persia, but the Jews had a great ability, it seems, to bloom where they were planted. And many of these Jews ended up prospering there in Persia as Joseph did in Egypt and Jacob did in Mesopotamia.

But in the days of the Persian Empire, God, by His mercy, allowed some of the Jews to return to Israel. Joshua and Zerubbabel led these Jews home to their native land. Many of them had to leave very prosperous lives in Persia. It would be the equivalent of a Park Avenue doctor in New York leaving his practice to go live in a kibbutz in Israel. They were a noble people, most of them returning to a land they had never seen. They wanted to go back to Jerusalem and rebuild the temple.

And so, tens of thousands of Jews gave up wealth and prosperity and comfort to live for something bigger—the glory of God. You can imagine that the people of mixed race who had moved into Judah didn't like this very much. Who were these people who had been gone for three generations, coming back and claiming the land? The two groups had some serious conflicts, much like what is happening today between Palestinians and Jews.

The current inhabitants wrote slanderous letters to the Persian government, arguing that the Israelites had always been a rebellious people: "Check the file and you'll see that they cause nothing but trouble" (see Ezra 4:11–16). The Persian authorities checked the files and saw that, sure enough, Israel had a history of covenant-breaking with different nations like the Assyrians and the Egyptians. So the government canceled any plans for allowing the Israelites to rebuild the temple.

Fifteen years pass, during which the Jews are not allowed to work on the temple. What do you think happened during that time? Remember these people had made an initial act of separation and consecration, leaving their prosperity and wealth for the great adventure of restoring God's land. So what did they do? They began to focus on themselves. They took their abilities, wealth, talents, savvy, and chutzpa and used them for their personal gain. They built fine paneled houses of wood, a precious commodity, while the house of God sat in disrepair. They went into Lebanon, brought down the best wood, and crafted it. But it wasn't for the house of God; it was for their own homes. They became worldly and lived like it for fifteen years.

God raised up a fellow named Haggai to be His prophet to the people. Haggai began his message to the people by saying, "Thus says the Lord of hosts" (Hag. 1:2).

"Lord of hosts" is an awesome name for God. It means "the God of the armies of the angelic realm." It is the God who is to be served by all of creation. It's the title for God in the book of Haggai, showing that He is lofty, grand, and marvelous.

What does this Lord of hosts say? "This people says, 'The time has not come, even the time for the house of the Lord to be rebuilt'" (Hag. 1:2).

Notice that God didn't say, "My people." He said, "This people." Why? Because, He said, "You are not living like my covenant people, you're not living like the people I chose and empowered and redeemed and freed. You're just like the heathen, no different. It's just that you're calling on Me to bless your little personal ambitions. You're not serving Me; you think I am serving you."

What was the people's excuse? The task before them was so difficult they believed it obviously could not be the will of God. Do we still use that excuse today? "It must not be God's timing because it's so hard. I quit." They said, "It's too difficult. I will not live for God in His temple, I will live for me and my temple, my house."

You can imagine God's response to this. Look at the sarcasm in it: "Is it time for you yourselves to dwell in your paneled houses, while [the house of God] lies desolate?" (Hag. 1:4). They said "the time has not yet come" to build the house of the Lord, so God asks them if the time has come for them to live in the lap of luxury while the temple is in disrepair.

Let me share what God says in the Tommy Nelson Texas Version: "I notice you don't have time to commit yourself to the temple. But you have plenty of time to cut down timber, pay for it, and craft it for your own pleasure and convenience."

Do you feel just a little bit convicted about your values? We are a people called by God, chosen by God, and commissioned by God. Too often we forsake that calling and live like the world.

He is saying to us through Haggai, "Check your values. You don't have energy and discipline for things of God. You don't sacrifice for Me, but you make incredible sacrifices for your own personal pleasures."

Discipline in the Things of God

When I first started in the ministry, I had an appointment with one of the college guys in the North Texas State group, a golfer. Driving around Denton, Texas, for the afternoon appointment involved going through an incredible sleet storm. The wind was blowing so hard the sleet was falling at about a forty-five-degree angle.

I passed by the golf course and noticed the college guy's car in the lot. I looked over at the driving range and saw him in the middle of the storm, hitting balls. I thought to myself, *What manner of man is this? He is out working on his golf game in the driving sleet.* I drove to my house and waited for him to arrive.

A few minutes later he showed up, drying himself with a towel. After a few preliminaries, he said, "Tom, can you help me? I got a problem I'm dealing with."

"Lay it on me!" I said.

"Tom, I have no discipline in my life."

I reacted like you're probably reacting right now. I laughed. Then I replied, "Brother, you are the most disciplined person I've ever seen in my life. Didn't I just see you out on the driving range, hitting sand wedges into the sleet to make sure that when you came up out of the trap in your next round, you'd not lose a stroke? Wasn't that you?"

"Yeah, I guess it was," he said.

"Let me tell you something straight," I began. "Your problem is not discipline; your problem is worldliness. You happen to be very disciplined in things that you care about. You're just not disciplined in the things of God."

That is true for all of us at one time or another. A man may say, "I can't have a quiet time," but that same man will go sit in a duck blind at 5:30 a.m. in the cold. (I know that from experience because I was there recently myself.) Everyone has the ability to be disciplined in the things they are passionate about. Haggai shows us that we are often more passionate about our own immediate pleasure than we are the glory of God.

Eventually, though, our time will run out. Look what God says to the Israelites through Haggai: "Consider your ways! You have sown much, but harvest little; you eat, but there is not enough to be satisfied; you drink, but there is not enough to become drunk" (Hag. 1:5–6).

God says, "Let's see how you've done. Have you actually grabbed the brass ring? Have you found Utopia?" Of course the reality is that the people had never been able to satisfy themselves. They didn't even have enough grapes to make wine.

God refused to bless the crops of the people. God was cursing the land, as He promised He would whenever the people committed idolatry. By living for themselves, the people were not practicing theological idolatry but practical idolatry—greed and selfishness.

So God tells them again, "Consider your ways! Go up to the mountains, bring wood and rebuild the temple, that I may be pleased with it and be glorified . . . . You look for much, but behold, it comes to little; when you bring it home, I blow it away" (Hag. 1:7–9).

You are not successful and you are not happy. And I want you to see that God takes full responsibility for this. He says, "I am the one who has cursed your life. I do not like how you are living and I cannot enable you to continue by blessing you. I am blowing your stuff away."

He says, "I'm the Lord of hosts. I own the universe and I will not let it cooperate with you. You will always have bad fortune."

God says He is going to keep up the pressure until His people realize they must serve Him rather than themselves. He's not going to let up. It's like that scene from *Cool Hand Luke* when Lucas Jackson (Paul Newman) is told he will be punished until "he gets his mind right." God says we have to get our minds right about our values.

You're the servant, God is the King, not vice versa. Is it possible for God to continually curse your life until you finally lift your gaze to what God wants you to do? Absolutely. There is a story from the Reformation that illustrates this point. It is said that John Calvin stopped in Geneva one night on his way to Strassburg. He met Guillaume Farel, the leader of the reformation in that city, and Farel asked Calvin to stay and help with the rising flame of the Reformation. Calvin declined: "I can't, I am going to Strassburg to live a quiet scholar's life." Do you know what Farel said to him? He said, "May God curse your studies if now in her time of need you refuse to lend your aid to His Church."

We need people in our lives like that, people willing to call us to account and check our values. Calvin repented and committed himself to the greater cause. Almost every Protestant church in America owes a great debt to John Calvin. His work lives on five hundred years after his death because he adjusted his values.

In Haggai, after the people repent of their sin, God says, "I am with you" (Hag. 1:13). God will turn your life around quickly and join you in your journeys when you get your values straight.

Getting Your Values Straight

You may be reading this book, thinking, *I've already gotten my values right. I'm living for God from the ends of my toes.* God bless you.

You also may be reading this book and realizing your values need some realignment. If I asked you what you've read in the Bible this month, you could not tell me. The reason you don't read it is because it is ammunition for a battle that you are not fighting. You don't value God's truth for your life; you think you can handle it on your own.

If I were to ask you who you've shared the gospel with, could you tell me? If I asked how long it has been since you've discipled someone, could you tell me?

And yet if you were applying for a job or a scholarship, you could give me a résumé of all your worldly accomplishments. Too many Christians are really no different than any pagan; it's just that they've got this little slip that will get them into glory.

Are you happy? Are your values correct? Maybe this chapter has shaken you up because you're not happy and your life feels empty. So what can you do to realign your values?

The first thing to do is check your motives during your day. As you work, think about why you are working and what you are hoping to accomplish. As you talk to friends, think about what is going on in your heart. Your motives will often expose your values. Pray and ask God to help you align your heart with His heart. Ask Him to help you do everything you do to the glory of God.

Second, tithe the best time of your day to God, to get alone with Him. I'd suggest getting a cup of coffee. In my opinion you ought to have some addictive substance with you to really study the Bible; it's just a rule. Take a pen and some paper and read a chapter of the Old Testament, a chapter of the New Testament, a psalm and eight verses of Proverbs. Learn of God! Then close your Bible and worship. Praise God for who He is and thank Him for what He has done for you.

Then pray for yourself, your spouse, your family, your church, your city, your state, our country, and the world. Pray for the souls of the men and women that God has put around you. Pray for God to grant you boldness to preach the gospel. Pray and confess the sins from the darkest recesses of your heart.

If you're like most people, the first three minutes of your prayer time will be hard, and you'll wish you hadn't started. But the last three will be so sweet you'll be sad to have it come to an end. Make time for God every single day and make that the best time of your day. On the first day of the week, the day that Jesus rose, go to church and sing, listen, and repent.

Then begin a dialogue with someone about how God is transforming your values. When you finish this chapter, I dare you to put this book down and talk to your spouse about your values. Ask them to help you think through what God wants to do in your life.

Taking the Right Next Step

God can change you, but you must begin by changing your mind. You need to envision a new future with God at the center rather than the world's standards at the center. Take the next step God has for you in your life. It may mean starting to attend church regularly. It may mean that you read your Bible and pray every day for a month. It may mean you join a small group Bible study that takes you deeper into Scripture and the things of God.

Your next step might be to start sharing your faith, to ask God to open doors each day for you to share with someone why you have placed your hope in Christ. It may be that your next step is to go on a mission trip that takes you out of your comfort zone. Or perhaps your next step is to take on a leadership role in your church, to give yourself to something of eternal value.

Invest your life; don't just spend it. Make ripples not just splashes. Align your values with God's.

Many times we don't have the correct values because we don't understand the reality of our situation. W. E. Sangster told this story.

> As the Titanic was sinking, a frightened woman found her place in one of the lifeboats that was about to be dropped into the raging North Atlantic. She thought suddenly of something she needed in light of the situation—death was breathing down her neck. She asked for permission to run to her state room. She was granted a few minutes with the warning that if she did not return in that period she would be left. She quickly ran across a deck already slanted at a danger- ous angle. She ran through the gambling room that had

money piled in one corner ankle deep. She came to her stateroom and pushed aside her boxes of jewelry and reached above her bed and got three small oranges and then ran for the lifeboat.

Death had boarded the Titanic and one blast of its breath had transformed all values. In that moment she preferred three small oranges to a crate of diamonds.[1]

We are living on a sinking ship. Our culture wants us to hunt for diamonds while the deck descends. Do you want to be successful in the things that don't matter? Or do you want to give God glory? Get your values straight; they determine your life.

Biblical success comes when you

1. give God the first of your time—a quiet thirty minutes of Bible reading, prayer, and meditation;
2. give God the first of your week—make Sunday worship a higher priority;
3. give God the first of your wealth—begin where you can and aim for at least 10 percent;
4. give God the first of your plans—think about what you will plan and do in the next year for Him.

These steps will shape your values, and your values will shape your life.

A PRAYER FOR TRUE SUCCESS

Father, thank You for the privilege of understanding what is ultimately true. Thank You for the birthright of being able to find true success. Sometimes we get off-kilter. We live like gerbils and goldfish. We don't savor and delight in the things of God. Help us, Lord. Only in the illumination of Your Word do we hear the echoes of the other side. We are besieged with error through friends, the television, magazines, and the world. We will pass fifty billboards today, none of which represents Your truth. Help us align our values with Your heart so we might find success. We ask this in Jesus' name. Amen.

THINKING MORE DEEPLY ABOUT TRUE SUCCESS

1. If you could write a one-sentence obituary for your life, what would you want it to say? Why?

2. Do you believe that "values are even more important than intelligence, gifts, abilities, and hard work"? Why or why not?

3. "Where your values are, your heart will follow." How have you seen this in your own life or the lives of people around you?

4. Have you ever realized that you said no to the wrong thing—that you invested too much of your soul into something that didn't really matter? What was that experience like? What did you learn?

5. If someone were to follow you around for a week, would they say you were committed to transcendent things? What would they say are the most important things in your life? Are these the things you want to give your life to? If not, what changes do you need to make?

CHAPTER 4

Integrity:

Matching Up Your Faith and Life

Years ago, a pastor in London got on a trolley. He bought his ticket, and the trolley driver gave him back an exorbitant amount of change. The pastor went and sat down in his chair, looked at the change, and realized what had happened. I'm sure his first thought was, *Praise the Lord. God has taken care of my bills.* But after he sat there for awhile, he thought, *Can my gain be another man's loss?* He went forward and said to the driver, "You gave me too much money; I'm sorry."

And the trolley driver looked at him and said, "I knew I gave you too much money. I was in your church last Sunday, and I heard you preaching on honesty. I just wanted to see if you were for real."[1]

After we build a foundation of the fear of God, establish good relationships, and get our values straight, the next building block for a successful life is integrity. And integrity is in short supply in our modern world. Consider the phrase "honest mechanic." Lots of people would consider that an oxymoron. How about a "truthful politician"? A lot of folks don't think that's possible. Many people lack integrity; they figure that everyone else must be like them.

You can lead a good life for awhile without integrity. You can have lots of people like you and get lots of stuff, but it will be a house of cards. Eventually, a lack of integrity will cause the façade of your life to collapse in a great heap. And it won't be pretty.

Solomon, who had a lot of silver and gold, said, "A good name is to be more desired than great wealth" (Prov. 22:1).

The Hebrew word for integrity, *tom*, is used thirty times in the Old Testament. It means "complete"—that there is no distinction between what you say and what you do. The Greek word *aphelotes* means "integrity" and "singleness." In English, you can see the meaning of the word by seeing how its root is used. *Integer* means "one," and integrating involves two things coming together as one. The opposite of integrity would be hypocrisy.

Simply put, integrity is doing what you said you would do. It is keeping your word and fulfilling your promise. It means that you don't wear a cross and claim to be a Christian while simultaneously being an abusive man or a disrespectful wife or an uninterested and uncaring parent. If you say you're a Christian, but in your job make a bad product, rebel against your boss, gossip, or act unethically, that is hypocrisy.

Are all the people you respect and esteem wealthy, handsome, and successful people, as the world defines success? Think about it for a few minutes. If you're like me, the people who have had the greatest impact on you are people of integrity. The Bible says, "The memory of the righteous is blessed, but the name of the wicked will rot" (Prov. 10:7).

Reputation Versus Integrity

Reputation is who people think you are, but integrity is who you really are. You cannot have a truly successful life if you are a hypocrite—it's just that simple. O. J. Simpson was arguably one of the top three running backs in football history. He was a two-time all-American, a Heisman Trophy winner, and the first guy to gain two thousand yards in a season. Yet no one will touch him today.

No one will have him endorse their products. Even though he has successfully acted in several movies, no one will use him as an actor. Even though he has a charismatic personality and good looks, he can't get work. Why? Because people believe he lacks integrity. We have heard the frantic 9-1-1 tapes from his wife when she accused him of beating her. And many people believe he killed his wife. He appeared to be one thing, but now people believe he is another. They see him as a hypocrite. He will live the rest of his life with the consequences of losing his integrity.

Contrast that with Michael Jordan, who is believed by many to be the greatest basketball player who ever lived. Even with worldwide acclaim for almost two decades, he has basically been known as a man who kept his word. A few years ago, many of the top players who were under contract held out until management gave them more money, but Michael Jordan never held out. He made less money than he could have. Asked why, he responded simply, "I gave my word!" For him it was an issue of integrity.

A similar story is told about Ted Williams. He was arguably the greatest left-handed hitter who ever lived. Do you know what impresses me most about Ted Williams? One year his batting average was under .300. That winter he sent back his contract and asked for less money. Did you get that? An athlete demanded less money because he said he didn't deserve his current salary. That's integrity.

You can live without fame, you can live without wealth, you can live without health, you can live without everything, but you cannot live without integrity; it will rot you from the inside. There is no true success without integrity.

Authors T. L. Haines and L. W. Yaggy said it this way: "Perish what may; perish gold, silver, houses, lands; let the winds of misfortune dash our vessel on the sunken rock, but let integrity be like the valued keepsake, the sailor boy lashed with the rope round his body, the only thing we care to save. Let one die; but let angels read, if friends cannot afford to erect the gravestone, 'Here lies an honest man!'"[2]

You are going to die. Your life will go down like a sinking ship. The only thing that you leave behind will be the memory of your integrity in the lives of the people in dark suits who attend your funeral. That's it! Your integrity is everything that you are.

Jesus and Integrity

What did Jesus say about integrity? One time Jewish leaders asked His disciple Peter about paying the temple tax. According to Exodus 30:13–14, every Jew over age twenty had to pony up for the upkeep of the temple. This was not an issue of Talmudic principles or of oral tradition (both of which Jesus scorned); this was a command straight from Scripture.

So those who collected the two-drachma tax came to Peter and tried to show that Jesus wasn't a person of integrity in this small area. (The world will still do that; people will find any tear in the fabric of your integrity.) They asked Peter, "Does your teacher not pay the two-drachma tax?" Peter said that Jesus did. "And when he came into the house, Jesus spoke to him first, saying, 'What do you think, Simon? From whom do the kings of the earth collect customs or poll-tax, from their sons or from strangers?'" (Matt. 17:24, 25).

To use today's references, Jesus was simply asking, "Does Prince Charles have to pay the tax on Buckingham Palace?" The answer is no because the prince is not a citizen; he's a son. So does Jesus have to pay the tax on the temple? No, because it's His house; it glorifies Him.

"When Peter said, 'From strangers,' Jesus said to him, 'Then the sons are exempt. However, *so that we do not offend them*, go to the sea and throw in a hook, and take the first fish that comes up; and when you open its mouth, you will find a shekel. Take that and give it to them for you and Me'" (Matt. 17:26–27, italics mine).

In essence, Jesus was saying, "Even though we aren't required to pay the tax, they think we are. So instead of causing a scandal and harming our integrity, we'll pay the tax. When you're talking about the glory of God, it actually does matter what people think. We don't even want to appear to be preaching one thing and doing another."

Jesus was not concerned only about His integrity but also the integrity of Peter, so the coin that was in the fish's mouth was enough to pay for both of them. He wanted to show that God is concerned about the integrity of His people in the smallest of things. People around us should not see duplicity in our lives.

Paul and Integrity

How did Paul apply integrity? On his journeys among the Gentile churches, Paul collected money to take back to Jerusalem for the Jewish Christians. Many of the Christians in Jerusalem had lost their jobs and been excommunicated from their families and social lives. They had no money and no immediate means to get any. And Israel was experiencing a famine. So Paul took up a collection (from the Macedonians, the Galatians, and the Corinthians). He said, "For if the Gentiles have shared in their spiritual things, they are indebted to minister to them also in material things" (Rom. 15:27).

It's interesting to see how Paul says they handled the money. "But thanks be to God who puts the same earnestness on your behalf in the heart of Titus. For he not only accepted our appeal, but being himself very earnest, he has gone to you of his own accord. We have sent along with him the brother whose fame in the things of the gospel has spread through all the churches; and not only this, but he has also been appointed by the churches to travel with us in this gracious work, which is being administered by us for the glory of the Lord Himself, and to show our readiness, taking precaution so that no one will discredit us in our administration of this generous gift; for we have regard for what is honorable, not only in the sight of the Lord, but also in the sight of men" (2 Cor. 8:16–21).

So Paul arranges it so that three people will carry this money to Jerusalem. Why would he do that? Is money that heavy?

Paul said he was "taking precaution." In the Greek, this term is the word *hupostello*, meaning "to lower your sail, to slow down your ship." When a ship was nearing shore, they had to bring down the sail to cut their speed; otherwise they could hit the shore and sink the ship.

That's why you send three men with the money. Paul was taking precaution against anyone being able to accuse them of a lack of integrity. To be discredited would mean that no one would believe them or their message of Jesus anymore.

It matters what people think when it comes to our integrity. You cannot be successful in life when people do not respect you.

And so Paul essentially says, "We will go out of our way and be very careful, so that we don't lose our integrity and our witness."

Your Integrity or Your Life?

Later Paul tells the Corinthians about his desire to glorify God above all things. Paul says that even though he had a right to accept money as an evangelist, he wouldn't do it. The farmer has the right to eat from his crops, a shepherd has the right to eat from his sheep, and those who serve in the temple have the right to eat from the temple. But Paul wouldn't accept money because he had to preach—he was compelled by the call of God. He supported himself so he could preach voluntarily. He considered that a solemn vow. And so he says in 1 Corinthians 9:15 that he would rather die than have someone be able to say that I said one thing and did another. Death before dishonor. Paul would rather have given up his life than lost his integrity by being caught in hypocrisy.

Another great biblical example is found in the Old Testament: Ezra. Ezra was a scribe and priest who set out to lead a group of people back from Persia to rebuild Jerusalem and the temple. This was a scary trip across hundreds of miles of foreign towns and villages. As they leave Persia, Ezra describes the preparation for their journey: "Then I proclaimed a fast there at the river of Ahava, that we might humble ourselves before our God to seek from Him a safe journey for us, our little ones, and all our possessions. For I was ashamed to request from the king troops and horsemen to protect us from the enemy on the way, because we had said to the king, 'The hand of our God is favorably disposed to all those who seek Him, but His power and His anger are against all those who forsake Him'" (Ezra 8:21–22).

The Ahava canal is the border between Persia and the surrounding nations. Ezra's integrity was important to him. He had told the king that God would protect them, so he couldn't ask for soldiers. He wasn't going to say one thing and then do another.

We need to be like Jesus, Paul, and Ezra when it comes to integrity. Let's cross every *t* and dot every *i*. In some Eastern cultures, when a man loses face, it is considered acceptable for that man to take his own life. There are cultures where people are unwilling to live if they have lost their integrity.

Integrity and Your Heart

In our hearts we know when we have lost our integrity. Your conscience may be pricking your heart even as you read this chapter. You may have gotten into some habits that have kept up appearances, but you know your heart is not whole any longer. It's nagging at you day after day, pointing to your lack of integrity. Imagine you are telling someone in a public setting that you are a follower of Jesus. Is there any person who, if they walked in the door, would make you feel ashamed because of what they know about you?

If you don't have integrity, it will affect your ability to be bold in doing whatever God has called you to do. "The wicked flee when no one is pursuing, but the righteous are bold as a lion" (Prov. 28:1).

There is a quote that has been attributed to Clarence McCartney, the great pastor of the First Presbyterian Church in Pittsburgh, Pennsylvania. "The better the man, the better the preacher. When he kneels by the bed of the dying or when he mounts the pulpit stairs, every self denial he has made, every Christian forbearance he has shown, every resistance to sin and temptation will come back to strengthen his arm and give conviction to his voice. Likewise, every evasion of duty, indulgence of self, every compromise with evil, and every unworthy thought, work, or deed will be there at the head of the pulpit stairs to meet the minister on Sunday morning to take the light from his eyes and the power from his blow and the ring from his voice and the joy from his heart."

You cannot minister when you know you are unfaithful. You cannot be bold at work in standing up for what is right if you don't have integrity. Once you start down the path of compromise with the world, each step gets easier and easier. Thus, when Israel went to battle, Joshua said, "Consecrate yourselves, for tomorrow the Lord will do wonders among you" (Josh. 3:5).

A lack of integrity also affects everyone around you. It's awfully difficult for a woman to respect a man who will profess Christ on Sunday but treat her with disrespect the other six days. It is tough for a child to live in a home where he hears talk about honoring God, but the practices he sees are all about satisfying self. That's one of the reasons children who grow up in Christian homes sometimes abandon the faith.

If you don't have integrity, you will also affect your usefulness to God. Paul said, "I thank Christ Jesus our Lord, who has strengthened me, because He considered me faithful, putting me into service" (1 Tim. 1:12). God will not use an unfaithful man. He is merciful and He is long-suffering, but He will eventually take out an unfaithful person and put them on a shelf.

Dr. Howard Hendricks, one of my professors at Dallas Theological Seminary, once said, "Gentlemen, we live in a world that is weary of words. We are buried with information, but they still are [like Diogenes], with candles, looking in Athens for an honest man somewhere."

Steps to Regaining Your Integrity

So what do we do? First, we need to realize that we all fall short of perfect integrity. Only one man can read this chapter and say, "No problem"—Jesus. The rest of us are trying to match our lives with the calling we've been given. We are holy in God's sight; let's try to live that way in our experience.

If you are doing reasonably well in the area of integrity, don't let that lull you into complacency. Ask God to continue to shape your heart and mind and give you a unity of purpose with Him.

If you are not doing so well, now is the time to stop and make it right. Too many Christians just keep going month after month, pretending that everything is OK. I know because even though I pastor a church filled with wonderful people, we are sinners like everyone else. And I hear the stories. I hear the children in our youth group who continually ask prayer for their parents. I hear the wives in my church who weep from the despair of being in a home with a man they do not respect. I hear the men in my church who have been excluded from positions of leadership because of a lack of integrity in their family obligations. I've had to counsel college students whose ministries were devastated when their lack of integrity was discovered.

One man came to our church, walked in the back door, saw one of the men who was ushering, made a U-turn and has never come back. Why? Because he had done business with the man in our congregation and felt he had gotten a raw deal.

What do you do if you are struggling with duplicity? Do what Jesus said to do. He said if you're at the altar presenting your offering and remember that your brother has something against you, leave your offering and go make it right. Be reconciled to your brother, then offer your praise or what have you to God.

Sometimes in life, you have to be like Jeremiah—you have to uproot before you can plant, you have to tear down before you can build. Pray and ask God to give you the heart of David, who said, "Search me, O God, and know my heart; try me and know my anxious thoughts; and see if there be any hurtful way in me, and lead me in the everlasting way" (Ps. 139:23–24) and "Let the words of my mouth and the meditation of my heart be acceptable in Your sight, O Lord, my rock and my Redeemer" (Ps. 19:14).

Integrity comes when we have unity between heart, mind, and life. Ask God to throw light into the shadows and draw you back to Himself in repentance and faith. "Let love be without hypocrisy. Abhor what is evil; cling to what is good" (Rom. 12:9).

Biblical success comes when you

1. have integrity and do what you say you will do,
2. remember that Jesus was concerned about us being people of integrity,
3. safeguard your integrity by avoiding temptation and compromising situations,
4. recognize that integrity begins with a heart that will not tolerate hypocrisy,
5. pray that God would keep you on a path of whole-hearted love for Him.

A PRAYER FOR TRUE SUCCESS

Father, we confess that often our hearts are divided. We frequently say one thing and do another. We need You to make us people of integrity—people whose hearts are committed to Your glory above all. Give us the grace to not be deceived by the idols and temptations of this world. Help us find true success by rooting out all hypocrisy in our lives. We want to be ruthlessly committed to integrity for Your honor and to the praise of Your grace. We ask this in Jesus' name. Amen.

THINKING MORE DEEPLY ABOUT TRUE SUCCESS

1. Can you think of some famous people who have everything going for them but integrity? What happened in their lives?

2. Think of some of the people who have had the greatest positive impact on your life. Were they people of integrity? How did their integrity influence you?

3. How did Jesus demonstrate His concern for integrity with the temple tax? Can you think of any modern parallels to this story (expense accounts, receiving too much change, etc.)? What are some places in your life where you have had to consciously choose to act with integrity? What have you chosen and why?

4. What safeguards did Paul put in place to guard his integrity when it came to money? Do you have areas of special temptation in your life? What safeguards could you put in place, and how could they help?

5. Without integrity, you can't be bold in doing what God has called you to do. Do you agree with that statement? Why or why not?

CHAPTER 5

Self-Control:

Subduing Your Flesh
through the Spirit

He was born in a log cabin in Oregon and named for the river of life from the famous novel *Siddhartha* by Hermann Hesse. His life ended outside the Viper Room, a trendy West Hollywood nightclub, in the wee hours of Halloween 1993. He was only twenty-three.

The oldest of five children of a hippie couple, River Phoenix was one of the most respected young actors of his generation. River and his siblings broke into show business at a young age, and he was soon helping to support his family, ultimately buying his parents a farm. In 1985, he starred in his first movie, *Stand by Me*. Then he played the son of an eccentric scientist (Harrison Ford) in *The Mosquito Coast*. He was nominated for an Oscar for his role in 1988's *Running on Empty*. He also played the young Indiana Jones in *Indiana Jones and the Last Crusade*. He later played a narcoleptic drug addict in *My Own Private Idaho*, winning the National Society of Film Critics' best-actor award.

To those who knew him, it seemed that River had strong convictions. Strict vegetarians, his family used solar energy to reduce their dependence on other forms of electricity. River also seemed to have life by the tail. He was taking a break from working on two new movies that October night.

You are probably asking, who killed River Phoenix at such a young age? The answer is, he did. Witnesses said that River was hardly noticed by passersby as he went into convulsions on the sidewalk outside the club. His life expired on a dirty curb in Hollywood as a result of a massive drug overdose.

The list of names could fill a chapter of this book and you would probably know every one: Mike Tyson, Lawrence Taylor, Pete Rose, Marilyn Monroe, Elvis Presley, Bill Clinton, and on and on. What do they have in common? They are all people who were greatly talented, greatly skilled, and had great promise in life. Yet they did not possess one important characteristic: self-control. Their passions led them to dishonor, disaster, and even death. All because they chose not to control their actions.

What do you need to find true biblical success? Since we are in the fifth chapter of this book, let's start making a list:

a foundation of fearing God and gathering wisdom

the ability to maintain relationships

values

integrity

self-control

For twenty-five years I have pastored people who failed in life because they lacked self-control. I'll meet with them and find out they have taken four steps forward in their walk with Christ. Then within a few weeks, I'll hear that they have taken ten steps back. It seems like they are going to make it, and then life comes crashing down again because they will not exercise self-control.

"Like a city that is broken into and without walls is a man who has no control over his spirit" (Prov. 25:28). In ancient times, a city without walls could not be defended. Even if you had the strongest warriors, the best weapons, and wonderful generals, if you didn't have walls, sooner or later you were going to die.

The same thing is true for a man or woman without self-control. It may come now or it may come later, but you're dead if you have no control over your body.

"I discipline my body and make it my slave," Paul said, "so that, after I have preached to others, I myself will not be disqualified" (1 Cor. 9:27). Paul was afraid of what his body could do. When we allow our lusts and desires to rage out of control, we should be afraid of where they will lead—we should be very afraid.

Paul also said, "The fruit of the Spirit is love, joy, peace, patience, kindness, goodness, faithfulness, gentleness, self-control" (Gal. 5:22–23). The Spirit gives us the ability to gain victory over our flesh.

We discussed this briefly already, but it needs repeating: left unchecked, the desires of your flesh will absolutely ruin your life. You'll be left bloodied and battered on the side of the road like an armadillo that's met a semi. You cannot succeed if you don't control the passions that can ultimately destroy you.

Some of these uncontrolled passions are obvious in life: a man who repeatedly views pornography or falls into adultery, a woman who fantasizes about a romance with another man, a person who wields a wicked tongue. Sometimes these passions are more subtle and difficult to diagnose. It may be impatience and an inability to deal with circumstances, bringing on depression and worry. It may be materialism that makes you a slave to work and current fashion. It may be that you are too lazy to finish what you start. It may be a critical spirit that always seeks the fault in others. It may be a problem with authority, the inability to give affection, or a lack of forgiveness.

The Bible says these things come from our flesh. Paul calls it the "body of our humble state" (Phil. 3:21) and "the body of this death" (Rom. 7:24). Left unchecked, it will humiliate you.

In his book *The Great Divorce*, C. S. Lewis describes the flesh as a lizard that sits on your shoulder and whispers filth continually into your ear. Francis of Assisi called the body "Brother Ass (donkey)." Francis Sinatra, that other great theologian of Rome, said, "Your body is the monkey that is never gone, just waiting its turn."

Your flesh is hostile to God, and you will never be rid of it this side of death. It is like a constant hangnail. It impedes your progress.

It's important to note that the flesh is not an equal and opposite force. It has been dethroned in your life as a Christian. The flesh has been crucified with Christ. Its power is broken by the new covenant in the power of the Holy Spirit. But the flesh is still present. It is a live grenade. It is a pit, a loaded gun, nitroglycerin. It is a rattler always ready to strike.

No academic degree can help you conquer the flesh. No amount of IQ will do it. No physical prowess, no talent, no beauty, no accomplishments will help you put it to death. No emotional or spiritual experience will give you an ultimate victory.

The flesh is impervious to all those things. It will mock every single thing about you except the Word of God and the cross. Just like Roy Hobbs in the movie *The Natural*, who, with all of his great ability, had an Achilles' heel—lust—that destroyed him.

Marc Antony—a statesmen, politician, and warrior—was also heinously immoral. On one occasion one of his generals said to him, "Oh, Marcus, thou colossal child, able to conquer the world but you cannot resist temptation."

I have watched professors at seminary destroy their ministry because of their flesh. And often they were so deceived they went forward even completely understanding the consequences of what they were doing. I have watched well-known authors remove themselves from credibility because of their flesh. I have watched Christian musicians sing of the glories of God and then lose their ministry and their living because of their flesh. I have watched men and women lose friend after friend because of their inability to control their mouths. A lot of these people could quote all the verses in the Bible about the tongue, but at the time of their temptation, they couldn't actually deal with their flesh. I have watched men in my church—who through adultery, pornography, anger, or illegal business practices—ruin their lives by their inability to deal with their flesh.

My guess is that you know some folks like this as well. So why do I go through a list like this? Because it is easy for us to forget how dangerous our flesh really is. It's easy to forget that we can lose everything in only a moment. Alternatively, the person with self-control is blessed. The Bible says, "The hand of the diligent will rule, but the slack hand will be put to forced labor" (Prov. 12:24).

The first time that the word *sin* is mentioned in the Bible is in Genesis 4 after God rejects Cain's sacrifice. God refused his sacrifice because he wanted Cain to deal with his heart. God says to Cain, "If you do well, will not your countenance be lifted up? And if you do not do well, sin is crouching at the door; and its desire is for you, but you must master it" (Gen. 4:7).

God says that sin is like a predator. That Hebrew word *tes-huqah* implies to consume, to eat someone alive. In other words, God is saying, "Cain, your body will not peacefully coexist with sin and temptation. Your flesh will devour you or you will sub-due it, but you will not peacefully coexist. One of you has got to win."

A recovering alcoholic cannot coexist in a house with a shot glass. If he tries to peacefully coexist with alcohol, it will destroy him. He either masters the alcohol or the alcohol masters him. That's the way sin is. There's no peaceful coexistence.

I feel like I understand this text very well because I at-tended a seminary where I was taught this text by one of the five greatest living Hebrew scholars. He taught me the meaning of this passage just before he went out and had an affair. I was also warned by one of the finest Christian educators, who then proceeded to have an adulterous relationship. It doesn't matter who you are; there are no free passes. Every person has to deal with their flesh.

How do you deal with the flesh and develop self-control? Here are nine things the Bible teaches that will help you subdue your flesh through the Spirit.

1. Understand the Risk

You have to believe that you are at risk. The day that you think you are not susceptible to destroying your life is the day your decline starts. I have a friend in North Carolina who asked Billy Graham a question: "Billy, you have faithfully ministered for half a century—how do you do it?" And Billy replied, "I walk scared, young man, I walk scared."

Another great source of truth, the "Frank and Earnest" comic strip, summed up this theme well. One character says to the other, "Why is it that opportunity knocks once, but temptation beats on my door every day?"

And that's the way life is. Every single day we have to deal with our bodies. I have had a number of people say to me, "I thought it could never happen to me." Go ahead and circle it on your calendar; the day you say something like that is the day your fate is sealed.

2. See Your Sin in Light of the Bible

You have to illumine your sin in the light of the Bible. "The wisdom of the sensible is to understand his way, but the foolishness of fools is deceit" (Prov. 14:8). We need to see what we're doing and strive for righteousness.

Righteous men practice godly introspection. They get brutally honest about their sin. Godly women don't try to explain away their sinful actions; they walk in the light, not in darkness. "Search me, O God, and know my heart; try me and know my anxious thoughts; and see if there be any hurtful way in me, and lead me in the everlasting way" (Ps. 139:23–24).

"Let the words of my mouth and the meditation of my heart be acceptable in Your sight, O Lord, my rock and my Redeemer" (Ps. 19:14).

That's what it means to walk in the light. That's what it means to be filled with the Holy Spirit. It's our nature to cover up, but instead we open ourselves to the searing heat of God's truth. Self-control comes as we are convicted in the presence of God.

Our natural reaction to being exposed in the presence of God is to run, hide, and make excuses. After Adam sinned, he hid. God came and said, "Adam, where are you?" After Adam came back into God's presence, he explained his actions by saying it was the woman's fault. "And by the way, God, You gave her to me." Translation: "I'm not responsible for my evil; it was my environment and my mate, not me."

One of my favorite stories from the Bible is that of Aaron and the golden calf. Moses came down from the mountain where he had been communing with God and asked Aaron where the golden calf idol in the Israelite camp came from. Aaron stumbled over himself, reeling off the excuses: "The people are rebellious. You were gone so long on that mountain. The people came to me because of their sin and asked me to make a calf, so I took the gold and threw it in the fire and out came this calf." Isn't that great? That's the high priest of Israel! Sounds like some of the things we hear from children. Question: "Why is your brother lying on the ground with a bloody head? And why is there a candlestick beside him?" Answer: "I don't know! I think maybe a meteor hit him."

That's the way we are. One of the first steps to developing self-control is to be willing to acknowledge your sin. That is why, once a month at our church, we have communion. At every communion service, I ask people to examine themselves (2 Cor. 13:5). Are you dealing with your sin? You'll never develop self-control unless you squarely face the reality of your rebellion against God.

3. Remember, Sin Is Defeated

I am a Christian optimist. I know biblically that those who belong to Christ Jesus have crucified the flesh with its passions and desires. As previously mentioned, the flesh is not an equal and opposite force. By my new birth with Jesus Christ, who conquered sin and rose from the dead, I now have power over my flesh through the Spirit. It does not inevitably have to destroy me. I have a different voice and a different conscience. By the victory secured through the death and resurrection of Christ, I don't have to submit to the flesh. I am in an alliance with Someone who is victorious. That's why you need to reckon yourself dead to sin but alive to God in Christ. Calvary becomes our base of operations. As long as I am living at the foot of the cross by faith in Christ, my flesh is dead. I don't have to go along with it.

4. Crush the Flesh with Truth

Whenever you feel the inevitable inclinations of your flesh, stop them with truth. That's one of the purposes of the Bible—it crushes error. The Holy Spirit uses God's Word to interrupt the train of thoughts and feelings that lead us astray.

For years, standard practice for people with epilepsy involved treatment with drugs or even surgery for patients who have severe cases. But now, one of the most promising new areas of research involves interrupting the signals in the brain that trigger the seizures. One of these new devices is a vagus nerve stimulator. Similar to a pacemaker, this small device is implanted under the skin near your collarbone with a wire that connects to the vagus nerve in your neck. The device produces weak electrical signals that travel along the vagus nerve to your brain at regular intervals. These signals help block the electrical bursts in the brain that cause seizures.

The Bible does the same thing, blocking the messages of the flesh that attempt to dominate your brain. The Bible is a different voice than your flesh. It shows you that you don't have to sin, that there is a fork in the road where you can submit to God, resist the devil, and watch him flee.

An acquaintance went to another city on a business trip. Walking out of his hotel one evening, he passed by a topless bar. A young woman in front of the bar was trying to convince him to go in. He had the desires that every man feels, but as the temptation began to grow, he remembered the words of a hymn: "I would be true for there are those who trust me. I would be pure for there are those who care."[1]

The words brought to his mind that he wouldn't be the only one affected by his sin. He realized that his entire family, loved ones, parents, and in-laws—all of them—would be affected by his choice. It stopped him cold. Truth crushed his flesh. That's why you memorize Scripture.

In the Old Testament, King Saul wanted to kill David and was hunting him throughout the countryside. David was hiding out in a cave when Saul came into that very cave to relieve himself. David's friends told him, "Kill Saul! God has delivered him into your hand."

They gave him logic. They gave him peer pressure. David's flesh said, "Kill Saul," but he didn't. Instead he said, "Far be it from me because of the Lord that I should do this thing to my lord, the Lord's anointed" (1 Sam. 24:6). That reminder of God's anointing was all David needed. He was not about to thwart God's work in Saul's life. David knew he needed to be obedient to God because disobedience, as he discovered later in his tryst with Bathsheba, harmed not only him but the people of God's nation. No matter what your flesh claims to the contrary, you are never the lone recipient in the consequences of your disobedience. Others are always effected.

5. Fight the Flesh

After you crush the flesh, then you fight it because as its inclinations continue so your struggle continues. Consider these verses:

"Therefore I run in such a way, as not without aim; I box in such a way, as not beating the air; but I discipline my body and make it my slave, so that, after I have preached to others, I myself will not be disqualified" (1 Cor. 9:26–27).

"On the other hand, discipline yourself for the purpose of godliness; for bodily discipline is only of little profit, but godliness is profitable for all things, since it holds promise for the present life and also for the life to come" (1 Tim. 4:7–8).

"Therefore do not let sin reign in your mortal body so that you obey its lusts, and do not go on presenting the members of your body to sin as instruments of unrighteousness; but present yourselves to God as those alive from the dead, and your members as instruments of righteousness to God" (Rom. 6:12–13).

"Submit therefore to God. Resist the devil and he will flee from you" (James 4:7).

A great ice skater does not feel like getting out of bed at 4:00 a.m. to practice, but the prize beckons her. If you watch professional football, you'll see a whole passel of 330-pound linemen who can all squat 600 pounds and bench-press 400 pounds. If you have ever done the squat or the bench press, you know it is not an enjoyable activity. Why do they do it? They do it for the Super Bowl ring.

As previously mentioned, one of my professors at seminary was Dr. Howard Hendricks. He was also the chaplain of the Dallas Cowboys. On one occasion he asked Tom Landry what he considered the central purpose of his job. Landry replied, "My major role is to help these men do what they don't want to do, that they can attain what they're desperate to attain."

Every person wants to be happy, have a solid family, and feel that his life had eternal merit. Everyone wants to be a good mate and a good friend and have a good funeral. The only way to have that kind of success is to say no to your body. That is not always enjoyable, but you do it because the reward is greater than the sacrifice.

6. Starve the Flesh

Starve your body and its lusts. If you have a drinking problem, don't go have lunch at a bar and grill. "Make no provision for the flesh in regard to its lusts" (Rom. 13:14). If you are a man with cable TV and you have HBO, Showtime, or Cinemax (or "Skinemax" as some have called it), why don't you just also go ahead and put a sixteen-foot anaconda under your bed? It makes about as much sense.

In the last few years I have been counseling more and more people about the Internet. The Internet is just eating men and women up. Women are getting in chat rooms and finding men they can connect with emotionally. Men are getting involved in pornography and letting their lives get torn apart.

There's no way I personally will have any of that in my home. It's not because I am so pious; it's because I know I'm a fool and I know how badly I could fall. I've got a buddy who is a former alcoholic. He won't go to a convenience store to shop because even the smell of alcohol gets to him. Do you know why? Because his wife and family are more important than where he shops. Don't put yourself in the midst of something that can suck you down. "He who walks with wise men will be wise, but the companion of fools will suffer harm" (Prov. 13:20). Starve your body.

7. Feed Yourself with Wisdom from Good People

Don't just starve your body, surround yourself with wisdom. I personally try to put myself in the counsel of godly men that love me enough to tell me the truth. These men are not afraid to tell me when I'm getting off track. "A man of understanding will acquire wise counsel" (Prov. 1:5).

"Do not imitate what is evil, but what is good" (3 John 1:11). You will inevitably imitate one or the other. You will be affected by the water you swim in. Surround yourself with godly men. A wise man said, "Observation always modifies behavior." Sometimes we need accountability to others to help us when our faith grows weak.

Remember how Moses looked around before he killed the Egyptian (see Exodus 2:12)? "Is anybody watching me?" Have you ever had your phone ring when you are in an argument with your spouse or yelling at your kids? "Hello! God loves you! How can I help you today?" It's amazing how controlled we can be when someone is watching.

While many women tend to deepen relationships naturally, many men will want to stay shallow. They'll be buddies but won't be vulnerable; they'll be close but not accountable. Men have to work hard to present themselves to other men with the freedom to challenge them. But a man who won't do that will always be a weak man. He'll be a weak young buck in his twenties and a weak old geezer in his eighties. The only way to grow strong is to gather strong men to help.

8. Repent Quickly

Cleanse yourself as fast as you can when you sin. Notice that it's not "if" you sin but "when" you sin. We all fail and fall short of the glory of God, but "the blood of Jesus His Son cleanses us from all sin" (1 John 1:7). When you sin, stop right there and make it right. Remember the goal is not to be good enough for God to love you; it's to repent and come back to the cross where Jesus can be your righteousness.

What did your mother always tell you when you came in from playing outside? Wipe your feet. Jesus wants us to cleanse our feet—the part of us that walks through the day. This is why He said to His disciples, "If I do not wash you, you have no part with Me" (John 13:8).

Godly men and women are the ones who know how to stop and say, "Lord, forgive me." And they know how to go to another person and say, "Please forgive me for my sin against you." They immediately submit their heart and mind to God's Word instead of running from Him.

If you don't do this, you get a peculiar disease called "olfactory fatigue" that causes a serious disability. Olfactory fatigue happens when you smell something that stinks day after day after day. Pretty soon you can't smell it anymore.

I went backpacking with a bunch of guys to Durango, Colorado, for about six days. When the trip was over, we smelled like animals—we just stunk. But you know what? When you're with stinky guys long enough, you can't smell each other anymore. You're obnoxious to all of humanity, but you're with people who smell as bad as you do. If you don't deal with sin, an abnormal thing becomes very normal to you. Sin wears a groove in you, and you end up just following the rut and thinking everything is OK.

Near Dallas a few years ago, somebody shot a duck with an arrow. The point of the arrow went right through the duck but didn't kill him. The duck survived, walking around with an arrow through himself. It became a tourist attraction.

Too many Christians are like that duck. They are disfigured because they've learned to live so long with sin. When you mess up, you've got to have the character and humility to deal with it right then or it will disfigure you. If you don't, it is absolutely impossible for you to have a successful life. You will never have true happiness, true joy, or submit yourself fully in God's service.

If you don't deal with sin, you can learn to tolerate it. But the next step is even worse. You can actually learn to revel in your sin, craving it and wallowing in it to the point of being oblivious to the death it is pulling you toward.

Eskimos of the late 1800s had a particularly interesting way of hunting wolves. They took a hunting knife, dipped it in seal blood and then let it freeze. They repeated the process until they built up a thick layer of frozen blood covering the blade. Then they lodged it firmly in the ground with the blade sticking in the air.

When a wolf smelled the blood, he came and began to lick. As he licked, his tongue went numb even while he desired the blood more and more until finally he licked through the blood to the blade of the knife. He continued to lick, even after he slit his own tongue and began to taste his own fresh blood. His lust overwhelmed him, and he continued to lick that knife until he bled to death.

How do you catch a human? For a quarter of a century, I have watched Christians do the exact same thing. You may be reading this book now, but by the time the sun sets tonight you will go back to licking a knife. There are men who are consumed with pornography. There are women who have been trying to satisfy their emotional desires, and it's become so pleasing they can't turn back. There are young people who have gotten hooked on alcohol or drugs. There are adults who are compulsive shoppers. There are men who put sports above everything else. You can go so far down a path that you don't even realize the true consequences of your behavior.

Chuck Swindoll tells the story of a man who was mountain-climbing in the Sierra Mountains of California. In one particularly difficult section, he pulled himself on to a ledge only to find a six-foot timber rattlesnake looking at him with his mouth open and tail rattling. The man froze. The rattler struck, and the man moved so that the snake's fangs caught in his pullover. He could feel the snake trying to get loose beside his neck, so he reached back to grab the rattler's head. Unfortunately, he lost his balance and fell back, rolling down an incline with the six-foot rattler until his progress came to a halt on a ledge against a little bush.

Finding himself leaning over a precipice with a large rattlesnake wrapped around his head, he got a death grip on that snake's head and began to squeeze. He said later he could feel the hot venom dripping down his neck from the snake's fangs that were still caught in his pullover. He squeezed for a long time until he was sure the snake wasn't moving anymore. Keeping his death grip on the snake's head, he began to work the fangs out of his pullover. He unwound the snake from his head and kept squeezing. His hands seized up, so he decided to walk down the mountain with the snake. When he got back to camp, his buddies had to pry his fingers off the snake.

I remember Chuck looking out at us and saying, "There are some of you fellows right here who are feeling the hot venom on your neck right now. You have played with sin, and it is about to take you down."

Is there any sin that is so wonderful that it is worth your ministry? Your family? Your career? Is there? It's not enough to develop self-control to simply turn away from sin. You also have to realize what you turn to: the greatness and beauty of Jesus

Christ. It's not a sacrifice—it's giving up a burnt hamburger for a beautiful filet mignon.

Theologian Donald Grey Barnhouse talked about a buddy of his who was dating a woman he shouldn't have been dating. The war started, and he was gone for three years. During that time she found another man and married him. When he returned from the war, he found a godly woman and married her and was very happy. This buddy told Barnhouse that the first woman visited him at his house when his wife wasn't there. She came inside and made it very obvious that she was hoping they might get back together. He made the statement, "All I had to do was reach out and she was mine."

Barnhouse shares the rest of the story:

> There was within [the young man] something that goes with male desire, but there was something much more within him also, and he began to talk about the wonderful girl he had married. He showed pictures of his wife . . . praised his wife to the skies, acting as though he did not understand the obvious advances of the girl.
>
> It was not long before she left . . . . The young man was never more joyful in his life. He said that in that moment, all of the love between him and his wife was greater and more wonderful than ever. He could think of his wife in a clean, noble way. A philanderer might have scoffed at him, deriding him for "sacrificing" his pleasure, but there was not the slightest hint of sacrifice in the generally accepted sense of the word. There was, however, every sacrifice in the sense of his heart. The turning of his heart in mind and soul, yes, and even body to the love of his true wife was the living sacrifice

which praised her and made him all the more noble because of it. It is in this sense the believer in Jesus Christ presents his body a living sacrifice.[2]

Turn to the Greater Pleasure

Why does a man turn away? He turns away in light of the beauty of his wife. Why does a man or woman exercise self-control over their body? Because no pleasure is greater than the pleasure of bringing glory to Jesus Christ. No pleasure is so great that it should demand the price of your joy, your friendships, your family, and your ministry.

Sin is crouching at your door and you must master it. You cannot be successful in life without self-control over your passions, be they obvious or subtle.

The apostle Peter said, "Be on the alert. Your adversary, the devil, prowls around like a roaring lion, seeking someone to devour" (1 Pet. 5:8). But the apostle Paul wrote, "No temptation has overtaken you but such as is common to man; and God is faithful, who will not allow you to be tempted beyond what you are able, but with the temptation will provide the way of escape also, so that you will be able to endure it" (1 Cor. 10:13). We always have a means of escaping temptation. The Holy Spirit can so saturate your soul that He can help you gain self-control over your flesh and subdue it for the glory of Christ. Do this and you will find success.

Biblical success comes when you

1. understand the risks associated with the desires of your flesh,

2. see your sin as it really is in light of biblical truth,
3. remember that sin was conquered in the death of Jesus Christ,
4. crush the flesh with truth from the Word of God,
5. fight the desires of the flesh because the reward is greater than the sacrifice,
6. starve the flesh and do not feed its lusts,
7. feed yourself with wisdom from good people who help you love Christ more,
8. repent quickly when you lose self-control and find your heart wandering.

A Prayer for True Success

Father, we admit that we are weak-willed people who often go our own way. We lack self-control and are tossed this way and that by the desires of our flesh. Give us the grace to love You more than we love our own temporary pleasure. Help us turn away from short-term happiness to the greater joy of worshipping and serving You. We ask this in Jesus' name. Amen.

Thinking More Deeply about True Success

1. Have you ever taken "four steps forward and ten steps back"? What happened? How was a lack of self-control a part of that experience?

2. The flesh is always present, but its power has been broken by the death of Christ. What does this mean for your daily life? What competing truths do you need to remember to deal correctly with your flesh?

3. What is "olfactory fatigue"? Have you seen this in your life or in the lives of others? What steps can we take to keep from justifying our sin and allowing it to become a habit in our lives?

4. The Bible says we are actually turning away from sin to a greater pleasure—the pleasure of bringing glory and honor to Jesus Christ. Do you believe this? Why or why not? What difference should this truth make in your life?

CHAPTER 6

Submission to Authority:

Success in the Place God Plants You

In the early 1970s I was the chaplain of a high school football team. We love our high school football in Texas. We are connoisseurs of high school football. In other states they have high school football; in Texas, they live for high school football. For a whole bunch of folks it may as well be the state religion.

So to be a great player in Texas means you are doing something. And on the team I served was a young man who was the finest high school football player I have ever seen. He was one of only three athletes in the history of Texas to be a three-time high school all-American (meaning, he was a high school all-American as a sophomore!).

When he was ready to graduate, he had his choice of colleges. He picked a school whose previous running back was the runner-up for the Heisman Trophy. The question was not whether this young man would be good, but whether he was going to win the Heisman.

After he made his decision, I said to his high school coach, "What do you think? Will he win the Heisman someday?" His coach replied, "He'll never carry the ball in college."

I was shocked. "What do you mean?" I demanded. And he told me this young man had a character flaw that would eventually disqualify him. He knew that his college coaches would see it right away, and that would be the end of his career.

Well, this young man ended up attending four different colleges—he quit two and was kicked out of two. He finished without a degree. The last I heard he was living in a common-law marriage and struggling every step of the way.

What was the character flaw that the coach saw? "He cannot submit to authority. He cannot submit to his parents. He cannot submit to an employer. He cannot submit to a teacher." The coach told me, "We've carried him along for the sake of the ball club. But I assure you, he will not submit to his college coaches. His football career is done."

That coach could have just as easily quoted to me a verse from Proverbs: "The eye that mocks a father and scorns a mother, the ravens of the valley will pick it out" (Prov. 30:17).

Our list of attributes of a biblically successful person continues to grow:

a foundation of fearing God and gathering wisdom

the ability to maintain relationships

values

integrity

self-control

submission to authority

Submission Starts Early

When a child starts early in rebellion to his parents, his behaviors are often prophetic about where his life will end—as an unsubmissive sinner before God. He can't submit to the authority of God because he can't begin by submitting to the authority of his parents.

Every one of us has a problem with authority. As fallen humans we are like our father the devil, who said, "I will make myself like the Most High" (Isa. 14:14). He didn't want God telling him what to do. Our first sin in the garden of Eden was rebellion against authority. The serpent said, "Indeed, has God said, 'You shall not eat from any tree of the garden'? . . . God knows that in the day you eat from it your eyes will be opened, and you will be like God, knowing good and evil" (Gen. 3:1, 5).

The serpent told Adam and Eve that submission to authority would never allow them to become what they wanted to be. "To become all that you're supposed to be, you have to be a free spirit and rebel." This is the lie of the garden, and it's the lie of our culture as well.

That's why God so clearly commands us to be submissive wherever we are. We were transferred out of the kingdom of darkness into the kingdom of God's dear Son. It truly is His way or the highway. Talk about not being politically correct.

But the reality is that you cannot be successful in life when you are constantly fighting against the institutions around you. If you have constant friction and tumult against authority, you will never have success. As a child, parent, mate, employee, or citizen of a government, you cannot be successful and happy in life with an independent spirit in rebellion against authority.

So first we fix our values by cherishing what God cherishes. Then we gain integrity by uniting our heart to God's heart. Then we learn self-control by allowing God's Spirit to help us subdue the flesh. Now we submit to authority to gain success in the place God plants us.

Here are five things the Bible says about authority and about how we are to respond to it.

1. Everyone Has to Submit

Everybody has to submit to authority. No one is truly independent. "Children, obey your parents" (Eph. 6:1). "Wives, be subject to your own husbands," but then Paul says, "For the husband is the head of the wife, as Christ also is the head of the church" (Eph. 5:22, 23).

No man is independent. Men don't get to be independent from their wives—even though she is to submit to him—because before men are husbands, they are Christ's brides. If you're going to be any good as a husband, you have to be a bride first. The man who wants obedience yet will not give to God his own submission is called a "rogue mate."

Submit to those in positions of authority in your work world, "not only to those who are good and gentle, but also to those who are unreasonable" (1 Pet. 2:18). Do your best. We are to be good workers, not by "eyeservice, as men-pleasers, but as slaves of Christ, doing the will of God from the heart" (Eph. 6:6).

In every area of our lives, we are to submit to Christ. That means we are His servants. "Every person is to be in subjection to the governing authorities" (Rom. 13:1); we have to be submissive to government. In the church, younger men are to "be subject to your elders" (1 Pet. 5:5). "Appreciate those who diligently labor among you, and have charge over you in the Lord and give you instruction" (1 Thess. 5:12). You're to be submissive to a church structure. The Bible also says to "be subject to one another in the fear of Christ" (Eph. 5:21). Bob Dylan had it right in his gospel song, "Gotta Serve Somebody." We're servants to each other, and ultimately we submit to God.

So whether you are a child, a wife, a husband, a worker, a citizen, a human, or a Christian, all of us have to submit. When once I spoke in Washington, D.C., a congressmen's wife told me, "You work to get to this place by being good in your job and good in the law practice. You earn your way up, then you're in Congress and you're everybody's servant. Now we have about a million bosses." Nobody is independent.

2. God Demands Submission

Submission is a divine commandment. Paul is not laying down some arbitrary rules. "All right you kids, let's see . . . you be submissive to parents; wives, let's see, you have to do what he says . . . ." Paul is simply reflecting the nature of God Himself. Within the Trinity, there is submission. God is triune and even though the three Persons are equal, there's an order within the Trinity. The Father sends the Son—"My Father . . . is greater than all," Jesus said (John 10:29). He gives the Son, and the Son delights to do His will. Jesus said that He would send forth the Spirit (John 15:26). The Spirit proceeds from the Son. That's known as the doctrine of procession.

"Now I praise you because you remember me in everything and hold firmly to the traditions, just as I delivered them to you. But I want you to understand that Christ is the head of every man, and the man is the head of a woman, and God is the head of Christ" (1 Cor. 11:2–3).

Paul says that men are to be leaders in the structure of the local church (1 Tim. 3:1). Notice the reason he gives is not rooted in the cultural norms of that day but in the unchanging nature of God. Submission is an attribute of the Trinity. God the Father is the head of Christ.

Whenever a group of people work at anything—at home or on the job—the first thing you have to establish is who is in charge. You can't serve two masters. Somebody has to be recognized as the leader. You can't have harmony if you don't have order.

So God has order and harmony within the Trinity. Father, Son, and Holy Spirit have an order of submission to authority. The same is true in creation. There is order: the family submits to the father—the children to the mother, the wife to the husband—and all of them to government and to God. We speak of the universe as the "kosmos." *Kosmos* means "order" in Greek. All that exists is in order.

3. Jesus Submitted Perfectly

The ultimate example of submission to authority was seen in the nature of Jesus Christ. As a perfect man, He was perfectly submissive. The Bible says that as a child He continued in subjection to His parents (Luke 2:51). He rose in the synagogue to read, as was His custom—submitting to the authorities of His day. He said submit to your leaders as they sit in the seat of Moses; however, don't do as they do but as they say (Matt. 23:2, 3). "Render to Caesar the things that are Caesar's" (Mark 12:17).

And about God the Father, He said, "I have come down from heaven, not to do My own will, but the will of Him who sent

Me" (John 6:38). In every area of society Jesus found Himself in—among family, government officials, temple leaders, His holy Father—He was wonderfully submissive to authority.

4. Great People Submit

Can you think of a single great person who didn't submit to authority? There is no great man or great woman in the Bible that had a continuing problem with authority. In our culture we somehow see the antihero as great. The guy that rebels against authority and does his own thing is given worship and adulation. But you don't see that in the Bible.

Jacob had to submit to Laban, his father-in-law. He told Laban (in so many words), "Ten times you've changed my shepherding wages. I've borne the brunt of the loss of sheep myself. I was consumed by the heat of day and by the cold of the night. But I will still submit" (see Gen. 31:40, 41). He was submissive to his boss who wasn't really such a good guy.

Joseph was a good shepherd for his father. Joseph was a great manager for Potiphar who bought him in Egypt. Joseph was given the keys of the jail where he was incarcerated. Can you imagine that? A jailer giving a jailbird the keys. (It reminds me of what Andy does with Otis the drunk in Mayberry, but this wasn't television—it was a jail of the most powerful ruler in the world.) The jailer would have lost his life if anything had happened, but he recognized Joseph's submission and gave him the keys. When Joseph was elevated to be "prime minister" of Egypt, guess what? He was a faithful prime minister. It was a piece of cake because he had always been faithful.

Moses was faithful to Pharaoh. Moses was faithful to Jethro, his father-in-law, taking care of his sheep.

David was faithful to Jesse, his father. When his daddy told him to take food to his brothers, he did it. He was elevated to the position of court musician. He was faithful to Saul. Then he became Saul's armor bearer. He became Saul's general. And then when David became king, he had no problem being a good king because he had learned submission as a little boy. That's the man after God's own heart.

Elisha poured water on the hands of Elijah. Ruth was a great daughter-in-law to Naomi and became a great wife to Boaz. Esther was a great niece to her Uncle Mordecai, who took the place of her father in calling her to submit. And Mordecai himself was faithful to the king of Persia.

Daniel was faithful to Nebuchadnezzar, to Belshazzar, and then to the Persian kings. Nehemiah was faithful to Artaxerxes as a cupbearer. The Bible tells us he had never been unhappy in the presence of the king—he wasn't bringing his problems to work. We could go on and on.

No great man or woman in the Bible consistently had a rebellious spirit.

I have a special program in my church to train the next generation of leaders. I work with between thirty and forty young men every year. They come from all over the country and do three things with me for a year: they study with me every morning for an hour; they do an evangelism program once a week, learning the material themselves and then training others; and they all choose a ministry in which they serve—junior high or high school, college, singles, the elderly, vision ministry, jail ministry, inner-city, and so forth.

I tell them straight up that I'm not bringing them in to lead; I'm bringing them in to train them to serve. I say to them, "You're the gopher in these ministries. You're on the bottom of the food chain. You set up chairs. You vacuum. You make the phone calls. You make the photocopies."

Some of them wonder why I ask them to do this when they want to lead a church. I say, "Young fellows, any fool can tell everybody what to do, but only a great man can serve. Unless you serve, you will never, ever lead." Leadership's a piece of cake when you learn how to serve. There is no greatness without servanthood. There is no success without submission.

5. Lack of Submission Leads to Disaster

When I say, "Samson," who do you think of?

Do you think of the boy who was a Nazirite, holy from the womb? Do you think of the boy who was named by God Himself? Do you think of the boy who was anointed by God? Do you think of the kid who was divinely conceived to parents who couldn't have kids?

My guess is that you didn't think about any of those things. If you know the story, you thought of Delilah and of Samson being captured by the Philistines. You thought of the guy who had his eyes poked out. You thought of a guy who was humiliated, tied to a beam, and made to grind grain like an animal. You think of a man who died in the rubble of his enemies. What led him to such a disaster? "And Samson noticed a Philistine woman and he said unto his parents, 'Get her for me, for she looks good to me'" (Judg. 14:3).

Nothing changes does it? "Get her as a wife; she looks good." But that's a huge no-no. You don't marry outside the faith in Judaism. You don't do it in Christianity. But Samson did it.

Samson's father asked him if he couldn't pick from their relatives or at least someone in the nation of Israel (Judg. 14:3).

Samson's father is trying to exert his parental authority. "Son, you're outside the will of God and I, your father, am telling you to stop right here." See, Samson was coming to a railroad crossing, and this great big arm was coming down while alarms went off, saying, "Ding, ding, ding, ding, ding, ding, ding! Don't take a Philistine woman as your wife." What do you think Samson said? "Get her for me, for she looks good."

Samson just kept on saying the same thing. He walked right on by his parents' authority. He would not submit. At the end of his life he, Israel's strongest man and warrior, is blinded, grinding grain like an animal and completely humiliated.

When I say, "Absalom," who do you think of? Do you think of the man of whom it was said, "was no one as handsome as Absalom, so highly praised; from the sole of his foot to the crown of his head there was no defect in him" (2 Sam. 14:25). Is that who you think of?

If you know the story, you probably think of the man who was hung by his hair while Joab put three lances into his heart. Then Joab's ten armor bearers struck Absalom and killed him, threw his body into a pit, and raised a heap of stones over it to commemorate his evil (2 Sam. 18:9–17). Do you know why? Because Absalom did not submit to the authority of his father and of God; instead he rebelled against it. Absalom! Absalom!

When I say, "Saul," who do you think of? "That's the guy who was a head taller than all the other Jews, a mighty man of valor." Is that what you think? He committed suicide on the battlefield and was beheaded by the Philistines, who pinned his body to the wall of their city Beth-shan. Why? Because early in his life, Saul rebelled against God, disregarding His directions in annihilating the enemies of Israel. Samuel saw it and said to him, "To obey is better than sacrifice . . . for rebellion is as the sin of divination, and insubordination is as iniquity and idolatry" (1 Sam 15:22, 23).

Submission and Children

Remember the verse I quoted after the story of the high school football star? "The eye that mocks a father and scorns a mother, the ravens of the valley will pick it out" (Prov. 30:17).

Rebellion against authority is a harbinger of disaster. The Bible demonstrates that this rebellion starts early. If you are a parent, you are raising a kid that is a potential disaster. That's why the Bible says, "Foolishness is bound up in the heart of a child; the rod of discipline will remove it far from him" (Prov. 22:15).

"Discipline your son while there is hope, and do not desire his death" (Prov. 19:18). What does that mean? Within about ten years, he will physically outrun his mother, and within about fourteen years, he'll be able to take on his daddy. Discipline your kid when he is young, when there's hope for turning him around; don't desire his destruction by letting him run wild. Raising a kid is like raising a Siberian tiger cub; you have a very short period of time to get his attention. In a little while the cub will be capable of eating you and everything close to you. A lot of parents never learned that lesson and ended up pretty sorry.

A number of years ago, there was a precious girl in our congregation. She got married, had a boy, and named him after a great Christian author. She tried to raise him in the Lord. But this kid had a rebellious streak in him, and he began to do his own thing. He physically challenged his father. He mocked his mother. Now why does a child do that? Because when you're a kid, you get to play with a net. You can be lazy, sorry, and worthless because you don't have to make your own food and get a paycheck or be cast out in the snow. You play with the net of your parents under you.

One night he was going out with the friends whose company was forbidden by his mother. He literally laughed in her face and scorned her. He and his buddies went out partying and soon ran out of money. He wanted to be a tough guy, so he said, "I know an old fellow who keeps money in a can. He's kinda crazy and about seventy years old. I think we can get the money from him. Let's go talk to him and tell him we need his money. If he doesn't give it up, we'll scare him and get it from him."

He took his buddies into this trailer where the old man lived. To show his friends that he was a tough guy, he carried a knife. He told the old man he wanted his money, and the old man said, "No." They tried to take it and the old man got irate—he was a little bit crazy—and he started fighting the young boys. It turned out that the old man was a lot tougher than they thought. This boy pulls his knife to ward off that old man and sticks it in him. His knife hit the wrong thing and the old fellow died. Now that boy, who up until that time hadn't been driving long enough to get a ticket, was found guilty of murder at age seventeen. He was sentenced to life for murder and sent to prison.

Parole won't even be mentioned to him for twenty years. I wrote to him and you know what? God finally used all of this to break him. As he turned eighteen in prison, he realized he had his entire life ahead of him and he began to seek God.

I read the letter he wrote his parents, asking their forgiveness. He's now beginning to put his life together. As a matter of fact he said he was happier now in prison because at least he wasn't a slave of sin, just of the state, which is far better and far safer.

This boy has an IQ that is off the charts. He's got such a great mind that I've begun to write him and teach him in prison. He can have twenty books at a time, so I send him twenty books on theology, history, philosophy, the devotional life, and biographies. He'll read all twenty of them in a month or two—just consume them. Then he'll return them, and I'll send him another twenty.

That's a story that warms your heart until you stop and think that there is a good chance he will spend the rest of his life in jail. God can still use him. He can have a happy life that honors God, but it won't change the fact that he is going to be confined in an eight-by-twelve-foot space for thirty or more years—all because he did not learn to submit to authority as a young man.

Why? Because, "The eye that mocks a father and scorns a mother, the ravens of the valley will pick it out" (Prov. 30:17).

We all have a tendency to rebel against authority. It's like the common cold. We're all susceptible; there is no serum that keeps you from getting it. Any human being that is a sinner doesn't like authority. But if you don't have that rebellion broken by faith in Christ, the following three things will happen.

1. You Will Suffer Turmoil

Your home is going to be upset because without a submissive spirit you're going to be a contentious man or woman. "The contentions of a wife are a constant dripping" (Prov. 19:13). Many of the proverbs are attributed to King Solomon, who had seven hundred wives, so he should know. A contentious, rebellious wife is like a dripping faucet. "It is better to live in a corner of a roof"—which means play softball three nights a week—"than in a house shared with a contentious woman" (Prov. 21:9). "It is better to live in a desert land than with a contentious and vexing woman" (Prov. 21:19).

A similar thing happens with a man who will not submit to the authority of Christ. He will be a worthless husband and a bad father. "Like a charcoal to hot embers and wood to fire, so is a contentious man to kindle strife" (Prov. 26:21) and "he who is quick-tempered exalts folly" (Prov. 14:29). And if your children cannot submit to authority, they will hold your home hostage. "I'll create such trouble if you don't give me my way that I'll tear this home up." Rebellion against authority creates turmoil in a job, in the home, and in the government. Lack of submission leads to a life of tribulation.

2. You Will Lose Your Witness

"Keep your behavior excellent among the Gentiles, so that in the thing in which they slander you as evildoers, they may because of your good deeds, as they observe them, glorify God in the day of visitation" (1 Pet. 2:12). When you can't deal with authority, you can't speak a witness because people see that your words and your attitude don't match. "He may say he loves God, but it looks like all he loves is himself."

3. You Will Suffer Alienation

This is more pronounced in men, but it can happen to women as well. You move from job to job because you can't get along with your employers. Or you never get close to anybody because you always have to get your way. A man will move from wife to wife because he can't find a wife that will put up with his abusiveness and neglect. A woman won't have any close friends because she doesn't have a servant's heart.

Nothing is worse than seeing Christians who have a problem with authority. They think, *Because God is my authority, I don't have to do what anybody else says.* Do you know what kinds of churches suffer the most from this? I can say this because of where I pastor—Independent Bible churches. Rebellious people just love to come to our church. "We couldn't get along with the Baptists, the Methodists, or the Presbyterians, so we'll come here because you all are independent." Our church tends to collect excellent people or troublemakers. The vast majority of our folks are incredible, but we regularly attract habitual troublemakers who just can't get along with anybody. *I'll come over here where nobody will tell me what to do*, they think. And then they create all kinds of turmoil until they either get right with God or leave.

Some men become lone wolves. They become alienated from people because they can't submit to any authority. They bounce from friend to friend. There is no getting around it—you'll be a lonely person if you can't deal with authority. As previously quoted, "He who separates himself seeks his own desire" (Prov. 18:1).

You'll also become very arrogant. Why? Because a person who is unable to submit to the authority of men is not going to submit to the authority of God. You can't be humble. You can't be under the authority of God and rebel against men.

A rebellious Christian is an oxymoron. Eventually, either the rebellion or the Christianity will go. So, if the rebellion continues, people just move out west somewhere and get a job where they don't have to answer to anybody.

Others will try to make their sin into a virtue. "I don't have many friends because I always speak my mind." He's taking the fact that he is a rude buffoon and trying to make others believe he is bold in the Holy Ghost. He thinks he just speaks his mind. He thinks he's being uncompromising in his holiness. He is actually just sinful and rebellious. He thinks he alone is standing for the things of God. The truth is he has social body odor and nobody can stand to be around him. A rebellious spirit will ultimately make you crazy because you begin to call your evil a virtue.

When you start living in an unreal world, all kinds of bad things start to happen.

Rebellion within the Family

The biggest problem for a person who rebels against authority comes within the family structure. How does a rebellious man act after he marries and is in the position of authority? He becomes either negligent or abusive. You can't be a husband till you're a bride. You can't lead until you follow. You can't be great until you serve. You can't live until you die.

If you want the top rung but aren't willing to start on the bottom, watch out. A man like this becomes verbally abusive to his wife. Or he brings turmoil to his house by being shiftless and negligent. He can't raise his children in the Lord because they don't know how to submit to Him. And he becomes lackadaisical as a father or abusive and angry toward his kids. When you're a man and have a wife, now you have to be Jesus, laying your life down for a bride. When you have a kid, now you get to play God, the Father; you get to shape life. You better know Jesus and the Father very well before you're given this kind of clout.

A rebellious woman marries a man. God help him! Because she can't submit to the Lord, she's surely not about to submit to this man. So she begins to undermine his leadership and emasculate him every chance she gets. If she can dominate him, she's happy for awhile, until she realizes she no longer loves the man she's helped her husband to become. If she can't lead, she tries to whine or manipulate to get her way. Woe to the man who finds himself in a marriage like this.

If you're a young person and have a problem with Mommy and Daddy now, you will have a bigger problem later on. You'd be better off dealing with that root problem now, telling your parents, "I've sinned against heaven and you." Get straight with God, then get straight with your parents.

If you're older and have left behind a wake of broken relationships, you need to back up and straighten them out. If you realize your marriage has been in continual turmoil because of your refusal to submit to the authority of God in your home, you need to straighten that out as well.

You absolutely cannot be successful in life when there is friction and tumult caused by an independent and rebellious spirit.

Biblical success comes when you

1. realize you won't be successful in fighting against the institutions around you,
2. understand that submission to earthly authorities reflects a submission to God,
3. submit to the authority and lordship of Christ in every area of your life,
4. follow the example of Jesus who submitted perfectly to His Father in everything,
5. recognize that every great person was willing to submit,
6. learn how Christ breaks a rebellious spirit and replaces it with the joy of service and submission.

A PRAYER FOR TRUE SUCCESS

Father, would You teach us to love and honor You? We confess that we often take matters into our own hands, thinking that we know how to run our lives better than You. Break our spirits—not to crush us but to bring us life. We want to learn what it means to rest under Your authority, to know the lasting joy of submission and service. Draw our hearts to You and replace rebellion with peace. We ask this in Jesus' name. Amen.

THINKING MORE DEEPLY ABOUT TRUE SUCCESS

1. Have you ever had problems with authority? What did that look like? What lessons did you learn?

2. "Everyone has to submit to authority." What are the authorities in your life to which you have to submit? Which ones are the most difficult to honor? Why?

3. Why does God demand submission? How is there submission within God Himself?

4. "There is no greatness without servanthood." How have you seen this in your own life and in the lives of leaders who have had an impact on you?

5. Three consequences of rebellion are listed in this chapter. Which of these have you experienced? What did you learn?

CHAPTER 7

Difficult Times:

Rolling with the Punches of Life

In the early 1900s, automobiles became the mode of transportation. One of the risks associated with this new pastime was flat tires. Roads were more suited to wagons than they were to cars, and almost no car came with a spare tire. A young entrepreneur named August F. Meyer knew an opportunity when he saw one. It seemed logical to Meyer that, with all those flat tires, there should be quite a market for tire pumps to be carried in cars.

Meyer established the Brisk Blast Manufacturing Company in Monroe, Michigan. Soon, Brisk Blast was producing more than five thousand tire pumps a week. In 1919, Brisk Blast became the Monroe Automobile Equipment Manufacturing Company. Soon after, the company perfected the first self-oiled, single-barreled tire pump. Sales climbed to more than two million pumps a year.

By the mid-1920s, however, two important developments changed the nature of Monroe's business. Service stations started offering free air for refilling flat tires. And automobile manufacturers started building cars with spare tires as standard equipment.

Instead of giving up, Meyer and his team applied the technology of the single-barreled tire pump to a purpose no one else had yet envisioned: smoothing the ride for America's drivers. In 1926, the first Monroe Shock Eliminator was introduced. When placed between the axle and the body of the car, what was a tire pump became a shock absorber that helped create a smooth ride over rough roads.

I'm sure glad August Meyer came up with his invention because my wife and I enjoy taking car rides on Sunday afternoons. We go out on country roads outside of town. Normally, country roads can be hard to drive on because they are so uneven and bumpy, but we go because we enjoy the pretty scenery. It wouldn't be possible without the shock absorbers on our car that take the jolts of those roads. Each tire on our car has its own shock absorber, so that the entire frame of the car doesn't take the hit from every bump. The wheel moves up and down so the car doesn't have to.

This response to bumps and holes in the road is the only way you can find success and enjoy life. You enjoy life by having the ability to give and flex with the difficulties that come your way. You can't have biblical success if you cannot bend with the constant tumult of your life. If you are mastered by your circumstances, by the things you can't control, I don't care what kind of education you have or how well you marry or how good a job you have, you will be a neurotic person who can't enjoy life. You will not be able to enjoy God, and you'll probably make life miserable for everybody around you because you almost certainly will not suffer in silence.

So we can add to our list of attributes of a biblically successful person:

a foundation of fearing God and gathering wisdom
the ability to maintain relationships
values
integrity
self-control
submission to authority
shock absorbers to deal with difficult times

The Consequences of Unbelief

You've probably heard of Howard Hughes. He was one of the most successful businessmen who ever lived. But he died as a disturbed neurotic because he was a control freak who couldn't deal with the normal difficulties of life. As he aged, he found he couldn't control everything. He decided to put himself in a place where he believed life could not hurt him. He moved to Mexico and holed up in a condo. He had guards around twenty-four hours a day. Nobody was allowed to visit him. He stopped cutting his hair, his fingernails, and his toenails. He died a neurotic recluse who had lost all the joy in life. Life can be brutal; it will chew you up if you don't have shock absorbers.

Have you ever heard of a man named Robert Howard? Probably not, but you almost certainly know his famous alter ego. Robert Howard was from Cross Plains, Texas. A small man, he was a borderline schizophrenic. He lived in his own world, had few friends, didn't marry, lived with his mother, did odd jobs, and didn't relate well to people. His mother fell ill and went into a coma—the only friend he ever had—and when the nurse told him she would never recover, Robert Howard went home and fired a bullet into his brain. He was thirty years old.

When relatives went through his meager possessions, they found great bundles of writing. Robert had erected his own personal world in his imagination. In this world he was not a frightened young man from Cross Plains, Texas, who lived with his mother; he was a bold, strong, handsome adventurer who conquered kings and warriors. He knew no fear. He was loved by women. He was revered by men. He was the master of his domain. In this imaginary world, he was Conan the Barbarian. Millions and millions of dollars worth of Robert Howard's works have sold, all posthumously.

I have counseled people like Robert Howard. Some of them are agoraphobic, meaning they are afraid to go outside of their houses. They're usually people who have been hurt at some point in their lives, and out of that pain they erect a perfect existence around themselves. They want an environment they can control. Their houses are infinitely neat—nothing gets in, nothing harms them, nothing challenges them, nothing makes them afraid. But if they step outside and cross that welcome mat, they step into a world they can't control. They begin to become nauseated, hyperventilate, and then flee back into their houses. Often they will die alone in the confines of their home.

Dealing with an Unruly Life

For most of us, such fears are not so pronounced. Still, all of us have to deal with an unruly life. This world is loaded and unpredictable. When life doesn't behave, some people become fretful and frightened. Then they become angry and depressed, they withdraw, and they become bitter. I have watched people in my congregation commit emotional and social suicide when life doesn't behave. They withdraw in bitterness and never go outside of themselves anymore. I have watched people leave a congregation of three thousand people because one person was mean to them. They were unable to have a perfect existence so they withdrew. If your circumstances dictate your perspective on life, you'll never be happy. No amount of training, skills, or money will help you.

I know that life is tough—I've seen it all as a pastor. Can you imagine what it would be like to kiss your wife in the bedroom, go fix the coffee, and discover her dead body when you return to her? That happened in my congregation. Can you imagine walking down the street with your wife, noticing her feet begin to lag, then having her look at you and not recognize you? She had a stroke right on the sidewalk. That happened the same month in my congregation. Think about the horror of being kidnapped and raped. It happened the same year. A young man received a call from his father who is barely fifty, telling him he has terminal cancer. This came just days after his sister's best friend was killed in a car wreck. Last month a child ran away. Yesterday a man told me he lost his job without any warning at all. A man and woman were waiting for the blessed event of a child being born, but at nine months that child stopped moving because the umbilical cord was wrapped around his neck. He was stillborn.

These are tough events, but they are also real life. Life doesn't behave the way you want it to. It's not a fairy tale where everyone lives happily ever after. It's not a Burger King world where you can have it your way. Sometimes life just doesn't cooperate. Someday, the Bible says, we will have a world where there is no crime or pain or tears. But until that time, you better have good shock absorbers to handle the potholes.

I wish sometimes we could live in the make-believe world of some of the cable preachers, where you just claim this stuff and you never get sick, you have all the money in the world, and you can eat all day and never gain weight. That would be a tremendous existence. But we have to face the facts—it's true that "the sufferings of this present time are not worthy to be compared with the glory that is to be revealed" (Rom. 8:18), but we have to wait until the other side of death. Solomon put it like this: "I have taken all this to my heart and explain it that righteous men, wise men, and their deeds are in the hand of God. Man does not know whether it will be love or hatred; anything awaits him" (Eccles. 9:1).

Translation: No matter how godly or smart you are, you are not the master of your fate. Solomon goes on to say that "it is the same for all. There is one fate for the righteous and for the wicked" (Eccles. 9:2). What is that fate? Death.

How will you deal with life and not become neurotic, schizophrenic, or bitter or alienate everybody around you?

You need shock absorbers on all four tires. Here are four biblical shock absorbers that will help you deal with life in an uneven world. You may want to memorize these. Tattoo them on your body if you'd like. Do whatever it takes, but don't go through life without these shocks.

1. Believe in the Sovereignty of God

God is the chief ruler. He is "our Father who is in heaven" (Matt. 6:9) and the "King of kings" (Rev. 19:16). Satan has to go "roaming about on the earth and walking around on it" (Job 1:7) because he is not infinite. He is not omnipresent as God is.

"I am with you always" (Matt. 28:20). "Where can I flee from Your presence?" (Ps. 139:7). God's sovereignty is what sustained Joseph. He had a prophetic dream early in his life that his brothers would bow down to him. Yet he was thrown into a pit, sold into slavery, and ultimately forgotten in prison. For thirteen years that prophecy stood in Joseph's face to mock him. Imagine what it was like. God promised he would be exalted, and yet he was rotting away in jail. But he trusted God.

God's sovereignty means that you can be like Jacob—given a dream in which God appeared to him above a ladder crowded with angels ascending to and descending from heaven (Gen. 28:12). His message was that He would be with Jacob and would give him the land and the promises of his father. But Jacob first ended up working for twenty years for a wicked uncle who cheated him at every turn. But he kept trusting in His sovereignty.

God's sovereignty means you can be a little boy named David who was anointed by Samuel as the king of Israel. Years later David found himself hiding in a cave from the current king who wanted to kill him. But he continued to trust in the sovereignty of God.

It means you can be a man named Paul who was baptized by a man who said Paul would bear God's name before kings. Paul went to Jerusalem to preach, got thrown into jail, then into prison, got transferred as prisoner on a ship that sunk, got bitten by a snake on an island, then was thrown into prison at Rome where he finally got to preach. In the midst of all that, he kept on trusting God.

It means you can be the Son of God, yet you are denied, betrayed, tortured, executed, and put in a grave. But you trust that even on the other side of death, God the Father will vindicate His Word.

And it means that you can be a Christian, told that you are in Christ, that there is "no condemnation for those who are in Christ Jesus" (Rom. 8:1) and that "all things to work together for good to those who love God" (Rom. 8:28). And you can hurt and cry, yet you keep trusting that all things work together eventually for good. The sovereignty of God tells us that God is purposeful.

A professor of mine at seminary, Dr. Robert Lightner, took off in an airplane to go preach the gospel far outside of Texas. You might think that God would make sure everything went off without a hitch, but that didn't happen. The plane flipped on the runway. Dr. Lightner was so severely bruised and battered that his wife did not recognize him after the wreck.

One of the students asked Dr. Lightner, "Do you have any idea why God allowed that to happen?" Dr. Lightner gave a great reply: "I was taught things I did not know that I needed to learn." Sometimes that's the way life is. We're instructed by things that happen—most of which we would never choose.

I would love to tell you that, as a Christian, your life and everything about you is perfectly protected by God. Biblically, there is only one thing God won't touch—the righteousness you are clothed in for eternity with God in heaven. Everything else is fair game (see book of Job).

When children play tag here in Texas, they will often say the phrase "king's X" to call a time-out or to avoid being caught. Unfortunately, your life does not have a "king's X." You may die in the next year. I hope not, but there is no promise that you won't. I would like to tell you that nothing will ever happen to your husband, but the fact is that if you are a woman, you will likely bury your husband. I would like to tell you that your career is safe and sound, but there are no guarantees. I would love to tell you that that sweet baby you hold in your arms will never get sick or die, but he might and some will.

I'm certain that Abraham thought that nothing could happen to Isaac because it took so much time and labor for God to give him a son. Yet, God said, "Take now your son, your only son, whom you love, Isaac . . . and offer him as a burnt offering" (Gen. 22:2).

Isaac had to give up Jacob and Jacob had to give up Joseph and Joseph had to exchange Manasseh, his firstborn, for Ephraim. God always takes your best because God had to give up His best.

You can't take an area of your life, put a vault around it, and say, "God, You can't have it." You can keep nothing sacred from God. Actually, rather than trying to protect everything, we should release our cares to God because we know that the purposes of God are for our good. Even hard times will work perfectly within His will. So the first shock absorber for your life is an absolute confidence in the sovereignty of God. Trust that God is purposeful in what He does. No accidents will happen that are beyond His control.

2. Hope in God's Glory

It really is like Paul said: "the sufferings of this present time are not worthy to be compared with the glory that is to be revealed to us" (Rom. 8:18).

When we hope in God's glory, we can be like Stephen. Before he died, he "saw the heavens opened up and the Son of Man standing at the right hand of God." It means that if needed, you'll be able to say, "[I] have been distressed by various trials, so that the proof of [my] faith . . . may be found to result in praise and glory and honor at the revelation of Jesus Christ" (1 Pet. 1:6–7). It means our "momentary, light affliction is producing for us an eternal weight of glory far beyond all comparison" (2 Cor. 4:17). It means if "we suffer with Him . . . we may also be glorified with Him" (Rom. 8:17). The end of my Christian life will be glory.

Paul spoke of "having the desire to depart and be with Christ, for that is very much better" (Phil. 1:23). That is glory. This world is not the best of all worlds; it is the gateway to the best of all worlds, but beyond the veil is glory. And if I know that, I can make it.

Before he became such a famous personality, Dr. James Dobson worked in pediatrics. On one occasion he worked with a five-year-old boy who was dying of lung cancer. One day in his room, that little boy began to cry out, "Bells, I hear the bells." The nurse heard him and said to his mother, "I think your son is close to the end; he's beginning to hallucinate. He says he is hearing bells."

Dr. Dobson said the mother looked at the nurse and said, "He is not hallucinating. I told him that when his pain becomes so great that he can't breathe anymore, then he'll be in the presence of the bells of heaven. He hears heaven." The mother immediately went into his room.

Dr. Dobson poked his head in, and he heard this little boy speak to his mother of the bells. She held him in her arms, and they talked until he was gone and could hear the bells from the other side. That's what it means to live for the hope of glory.

3. Enjoy God's Gifts

Life is simply too difficult to waste any time. Enjoy right now. Carpe diem—"seize the day." Don't let the elusiveness of what might be, take you away from finding happiness in what is. Everything created by God is good; Paul said, nothing is to be rejected (1 Tim. 4:4). Ecclesiastes says seven times that we should enjoy eating and drinking, the wife of our youth, and the works of your hands, for God has approved them. Enjoy right now.

What does this mean? When I gave a message on this recently, I used the following illustration about my upcoming schedule and my perspective on enjoying God's gifts. I said, "I don't know if I will make it to next year. I hope I do, but I do know where I will be in about three hours. I will be at a party. Mr. Bernard Bourque, my assistant, is getting married and we're having a shower; and I'm going to join in with exceeding mirth and laugh him to death. It's going to be a blast. I and my fellows will gather about Mr. Bourque and enjoy his hour of turmoil, and I will eat cake and I will drink coffee and I will be with friends—if I can just make it until two o'clock. All last week I was in Dayton, Ohio, so tonight I'm taking out my exceedingly lovely wife. We'll have a date but not just any old date; I'm gonna bathe and brush my teeth. I will pull out the chair for her at an Italian restaurant where it's quiet, with candles on the table and a little Johnny Mathis in the air. I will hold her hand and look into her eyes and enjoy my wife.

"Maybe I'll make it to this weekend. If I do, I know where I'll be. I'm going to Knoxville, Tennessee, to watch my boy. He's going to be playing baseball for the St. Louis Cardinals farm club. I'll sit in the sun and get me a Snickers and a cold drink. When the umpire makes a bad call, I'll probably sin, then confess it. But I'll watch my kid play baseball.

"And after that I'm gonna go teach about nine hundred Texas Tech students about the Song of Solomon. God will make some lives right, and I will absolutely enjoy it. So, if I can make it to this weekend, that'll be great.

"When I get back, I will get to see my son and my daughter-in-law. I have never had any girls in my life except for my wife and my mother. Now I've got this beautiful little daughter-in-law named Amanda. What a blast! My son is the funniest guy I've ever been around, and he always makes me laugh. I will sit in the presence of Benjamin, and I will laugh and I will enjoy Amanda.

"September will soon come, and it will be dove season. For three dollars I'll get a box of shells and go with my brother, and we will sit out by a mesquite tree with a cold sodey pop and wait for the birds to come in. The limit is fifteen doves, so I'll get three boxes of shells; that way I can get my fifteen birds. On the way out to Throckmorton, Texas, and back, we'll listen to Gaither southern gospel on the radio and just laugh and have a great time. So if I can make it till September, it'll be fun."

I believe that's how I should view a life that I know will also be filled with tragedy and disaster. The Bible tells me God wants me to live my life, enjoying the moment.

Romans 8:38–39 says that "neither death, nor life, nor angels, nor principalities, nor things present, nor things to come, nor powers, nor height, nor depth, nor any other created thing, will be able to separate us from the love of God."

You don't know what's going to happen. I don't know what's going to happen. A lot of the guys who think they know what will happen, don't know what will happen because it hasn't happened.

I make a habit of talking to older men and women about what they've learned because they're the closest we have to authorities—both those who have done it right and those who have done it wrong. So when I ask them what they would do over again, they say, "You know all the stuff that I worried about? I can't remember what it was. I wish I hadn't worried about things I couldn't control. I wish I had enjoyed more things, like my wife, my kids, sunshine, flowers, food, family, and friends and quit pursuing all those brass rings. I wish I had enjoyed life."

Ambition can be a good thing. Goals can be one of the things God uses to motivate us. But they can also be a distraction from what's important. The pursuit is fun, but once you get there, you find you're not really anywhere if you've forsaken all the treasures along the way.

4. Trust in God's Presence

God is closer than my dilemmas and closer than my problems. Paul said, "The Spirit also helps our weakness; for we do not know how to pray as we should, but the Spirit Himself intercedes for us with groanings too deep for words" (Rom. 8:26).

We don't even know how to pray as we should, but He intercedes for us. He places burdens on my heart that I can't even speak aloud. The Spirit knows what He places there because He's the very mind of God. So in something that I thought I could control—prayer—He says, "You don't even know how to pray, but I'll help you." He shares our burdens. He's called the Helper. "I'll be with you. I'll take care of you in your storm-tossed boat. I know where you are and I'll come to you. You just step out there with Me, and I'll take you through it and get you to the other side."

In 1976, Mel Summerall started the church I pastor, Denton Bible Church. He started this church because he had a deep walk with God. What do you think he said was the most important thing in helping him find a deep relationship with God? The death of his child.

Mel had five children—four girls and one boy. One day, his youngest daughter got sick at 9:00 a.m. By 3:00 p.m. she was gone. She had a virus that attacked her heart.

Mel felt utterly helpless: on the day his daughter was dying, he couldn't do anything. Like a lot of men, he said, "I felt guilty for my child's death." It tore his heart up so badly he didn't know how to deal with it. Now, Mel would tell you that's what happens when you try to be the master of your own fate. He didn't have any shock absorbers, and that pothole was so big he couldn't climb out.

He'd seen men killed in World War II, stood in Depression soup lines, watched his daddy become an alcoholic and die—he'd been through it. But, he said, "I could not deal with the sight of my wife holding the body of my limp little girl." He came home from work each day and sat in his room until he got in the bed at 6:30 each night. He just went unconscious, feeling that the longer he could sleep the less he would hurt. One night some friends came over, and his wife, Patty, went out to visit with them in the den.

Mel couldn't talk to anybody, so he went to the bedroom, sat on the edge of the bed, and said, "God, I can't handle this." This was the only time it ever happened to him, but it was as if a voice from the very inner part of his being spoke to him and said, "I'm here. I'm with you!" That's all he needed to know—"I'm with you." Mel said it was like something physical was lifted off him and he was OK. He didn't know what happened, but I believe God intervened in a special way to let Mel know He was right there with him.

That's how you make it through life. Even though the winds and waves blow, there is One who is asleep in my boat who will not be roused at winds and waves. But when I say, "Master," He is up on His feet. Even in my flawed faith, He doesn't rebuke me; He rebukes the winds and the waves. He'll take care of me. Even at the point of death He will be with me in the same way He was with Stephen to take him through to the other side. Even though the waters on the Jordan may rise as high as your neck like in Bunyan's *Pilgrim's Progress*, He'll take you through it to the other side. That's belief in the presence of God.

I guess one of the more successful women of our day, humanly speaking, is Mary Tyler Moore. I recently saw a special on her—talk about a traumatic life. She was married as a teenager and then divorced. Her sister in college overdosed and died. Then Mary got married a second time and divorced. But she remarried the same guy and got divorced again—three marriages with two men. Then her son accidentally shot and killed himself. In her despair she turned to booze and became an alcoholic, got off of it, but contracted diabetes as a result of her drinking. Now the diabetes has affected her eyes, and there is a good chance she will be blind by the end of her life. All of this happened to Mary Tyler Moore who has, humanly speaking, led a charmed professional life. But her summary statement about her success is "none of us gets out of here without pain." You need shock absorbers to make it through life.

You can withdraw and try to stay away from pain, but you will have to withdraw from having a real life. Alfred Lord Tennyson said, "Tis better to have loved and lost, then never to have loved at all." It is better to live and take the slings and arrows of misfortune then to be a spiritual agoraphobic that can't get outside of your own life.

One of my heroes is thirteen-year-old Curt Meckel. Curt is the son of a good buddy of mine who lifts weights at my gym. Curt is about as close as I can get to a role model. Curt is physically and mentally disabled. He can't talk. He's a little bit fragile. He's just now getting to the place where he can go to the bathroom by himself. He can feed himself. He can hug you and love you.

What do I love so much about Curt? It's almost as if he doesn't have a sin nature. He is innocent and pure, and he loves people. You can be a big guy or a little guy, a female or a male, any race, any income, successful or a bum; it doesn't matter. If you hug Curt, Curt will hug you back. He can't tell you how he feels, so instead he cries out in delight.

Everyone around him takes care of him. He thinks the entire universe was made as his sandbox. Every person that meets him loves him. He's got great big eyes. If you ask him a question and he can figure it out, he'll give you a little double take. "Yeah, I know what you're saying." And if you say something that delights him, he cackles. I wish I could include it on a CD with this book; it would be worth the cover price just to hear it. When we go out to eat with him and get him a steak, after I cut his meat up, he'll work on that steak and—if it's a really good steak—the whole restaurant will know. "HEYAAAAH!!!"

He's just into that steak. If a country song comes on that he likes, he says, "HEYAAAAH!!!" He'll grab my wife's fingers, and they'll kind of dance around. "HEYAAAAH!!!" He'll start dancing. He loves water—loves sitting in a hot tub with water bubbling up on him. "HEYAAAAH!!!" He just cries out with delight.

When Curt wakes up in the morning, has his yogurt, and sits in his hot tub, he never worries about life. He doesn't know where his next meal is coming from, and he doesn't care. I'll tell you why he doesn't care—because his daddy loves him. His daddy is about six feet two and weighs about 280. His dad bench-presses 450 and squats about 600. He is some kind of big. His dad goes hunting in Africa. He brings back lions and tigers and bears, then has them mounted and put up on the walls of his house.

He is the ultimate man's man. And yet I watch him reach down with his big hands, lift this little boy, and put him on his lap. They talk. Curt knows that whatever happens, his daddy is the biggest, toughest, strongest fellow in the whole world. And his daddy happens to love him. Everything in his life is governed by his dad; nothing will happen outside of his control. Curt just squeals with glee.

That's the way we should live. Whatever comes your way, you sit with your Father, you enjoy Him, you love Him, you trust Him, you walk with Him. And if anything happens that you can't figure out, you just grab His big thumb and you hang on and let Him take you through it. Curt is a happy man. He has shock absorbers. You need them too.

Biblical success comes when you

1. have the ability to give and flex with the inevitable difficulties that come your way,
2. have an unshakable belief in the sovereignty of God,
3. put your hope in God's glory more than any temporary success,
4. enjoy the time and circumstances that God brings,
5. trust in the presence of God even in the darkest hours—hang on and He will bring you safely home.

A Prayer for True Success

Father, we didn't create ourselves; You made us. Thank You that You have forced us into an existence that can be alien and harsh. We are sometimes slow to learn that we're not that smart, we're not that strong, we're not that wise, and we're not that good. Help us know that we can trust You, we can enjoy You, and we can sit with You. May we learn that whatever comes our way, Your big hand is right there with us. We can wait on You and You'll take us through it. Teach us, God, to squeal with delight at the enjoyments of this day and to trust in You whatever tomorrow may hold. We ask it to the glory of Christ and to the blessedness and to the happiness of His people, in Jesus' name. Amen

THINKING MORE DEEPLY ABOUT TRUE SUCCESS

1. In what ways has your life been unruly and unpredictable? How have you reacted to these changing circumstances?

2. How can a belief in the sovereignty of God help you deal with turmoil and difficult circumstances? What are the obstacles to believing this in tough times? How can you overcome these obstacles?

3. What does it mean to hope in God's glory? Do you have this kind of attitude? Why or why not?

4. What keeps you from being able to truly enjoy God's gifts? Is there something you would like to change about your life, based on reading this chapter?

5. How have you felt God's presence during a difficult time? Was there a time when you felt God was distant from you? Why do you think that was? What was the difference between these two experiences?

CHAPTER 8

Peer Pressure:

Who Will You Allow to Influence Your Heart?

I wrote this book to help you find biblical success. My prayer is that when you have finished reading it, you'll have a good handle on God's promise for your life (spiritually speaking) if you follow His Word: "You will make your way prosperous, and then you will have success" (Josh. 1:8). One thing I can guarantee—if you don't learn the lesson of this chapter, you will never get that success.

Back in the 1970s North Texas State had a running back who was one of the best who ever played there. He broke most of the existing records and, besides being an incredible athlete, was a handsome young man who had a lovely young wife and a little baby. He finished up his senior year and was preparing for the professional draft. There wasn't any question he would be drafted; it was simply a matter of whether he was going to be rich or filthy rich.

Before the draft, some of his old buddies from his former life came to visit. They were a far cry from him in terms of excellence, diligence, discipline, and ambition, but they were still his buddies. They asked him to go out to a bar. He thought that a father and a husband had no business in a bar, but his buddies pressured him so he went. At the bar, things happened that inevitably occur when you get people drinking. A fight broke out, and a couple of guys asked his buddies to step outside. Once out there, a couple of other guys jumped in, and this young man felt like he should step in to help his old buddies. In the middle of the fight, one of the other men pulled a knife, stabbing and killing him.

So at the ripe old age of twenty-two, his wife became a widow and his child became an orphan. This young man who was on his way, who had no limits to what he could become, was gone in an instant.

Why? Even though he knew better, he gave in to peer pressure.

Positive Peer Pressure

If you know anything about professional baseball, you know the names Don Baylor and Curt Gibson. Teams often signed Don Baylor and Curt Gibson to contracts as free agents even though they were past their best playing days. In the case of Curt Gibson, his back was so bad he could barely swing a bat, yet teams would still sign him.

Why were teams so interested in these old players? Because between those two men were about five World Series. They knew what it took to win. They were proven winners. Teams would sign them just to have them on their bench and in the locker room because of positive peer pressure. They pressured everyone around them to be better. They had never developed the habit of losing. They were totally intolerant of losing and losing people on their teams. To play with Don Baylor or Curt Gibson, you had to raise your game to their level. Teams were actually turned around because these men pressured everybody positively.

Back in the 1970s it was a known fact that when you signed with the Dallas Cowboys, you were a better player as soon as you walked on the field. Why? Because you had to play with people like Randy White, Roger Staubach, and Tony Dorsett. Those men didn't know how to lose. They were intolerant of people who didn't give their best. You became better as soon as you walked on the field because of peer pressure.

To continue the athletic illustrations, Paul "Bear" Bryant, who coached at the University of Alabama, said it best: "If you are going to be a winner, you must surround yourself with winners."

He understood peer pressure. Now, Bryant wasn't quoting Solomon, but he could have. Solomon said it like this: "He who walks with wise men will be wise, but the companion of fools will suffer harm" (Prov. 13:20).

It's an axiom: when you surround yourself with great men, you get influenced, and when you surround yourself with fools, you get influenced. John put it like this: "Do not imitate what is evil, but what is good" (3 John 1:11).

It's not a question of whether you're going to be pressured; it's which direction you'd like to be pressured toward. All of us are going to deal with peer pressure. Even Solomon took many foreign wives for himself, and they turned his heart away from the Lord so that he served their idols (1 Kings 11:1–10).

The man who wrote about peer pressure got pressured.

It happened to other kings of Israel as well. Joash the king served the Lord all the days of Jehoiada the priest. But when

Jehoiada died, the wicked elders of Judah bowed down to the king and he listened to them, abandoning God for idols (2 Chron. 24:15–18). Peer pressure!

How does this fit in a series about success? You cannot be successful in life when you surround yourself with people who are not. You have to be very selective who you allow close to you because they get your ear.

So we can expand our list of attributes of a biblically successful person:

a foundation of fearing God and gathering wisdom
the ability to maintain relationships
values
integrity
self-control
submission to authority
shock absorbers to deal with difficult times
positive peer pressure

Peer Pressure and Youth

We've all seen this with youth. A kid goes to a youth group, enjoys it, then learns all the youth songs. He goes to the lunchroom, gets pressured, and a kind of moral shyness takes over. He doesn't like standing alone—none of us does—and he gives in to the majority. A college student can enjoy the college service and learn his Bible, but he goes to a classroom where the gospel is scorned, Christ is assailed, and he goes down the tubes. He's afraid to stand up because of moral shyness.

It's not just with kids; I see it all the time with adults in my congregation. If a married couple comes to me and says they are separating, I will say to the spouse who is leaving, "Tell me the name of the third party you've been talking to." Generally, there is somebody telling them, "There's no way I would live with that worthless person. I would leave them in a heartbeat." Even though the Bible says to be reconciled to one another, that truth is shoved aside because of peer pressure. A fifty-year-old man or woman can leave their spouse because of peer pressure.

Here's another typical scenario. A young couple with a solid background gets married, and it looks like they will have a great life. The man gets a job in which he is surrounded by peers who live a little faster lifestyle. The man starts feeling the pressure. His heart begins to grow cold toward his wife. The things of God that brought him thus far start to be forsaken because of the glitz of peer pressure. I have watched more than one fifty-year-old man make a fool of himself. I know men who have counseled their children for years to stand against the tide and not yield, then cave in themselves to peer pressure.

All of us are susceptible. "All of us like sheep have gone astray, each of us has turned to his own way" (Isa. 53:6). That's why we do it; we're sheep. In John 10 Jesus said that we're His sheep, but we can still choose to follow evil or good. All of us get pressured.

Mike Tyson was arrested thirty-eight times before he was thirteen years of age. Thirty-eight times! He had no father. He grew up on the street, and his life was a mess. But there was a brief time in Mike Tyson's life that he was a model of good behavior. When was that? When an old guy named Cus D'Amato became his legal guardian and took Mike Tyson into his house. Cus and his wife loved Mike. And they found out that Mike could become a pretty good kid until Cus died and a fellow named Don King stepped in and Mike Tyson went down the tubes. Peer pressure!

Peer pressure can also work in good ways. A friend of mine named Jerry Campbell ran a youth home called Youth for Tomorrow. It was the greatest youth home I've ever seen, and I've seen a bunch of them. He took these problem boys and surrounded them with great godly men and women in his home. He enforced a standard of righteousness. He didn't give them an option. He was a Marine lieutenant in Vietnam, so he had some clout with the boys. Jerry surrounded these kids with righteousness.

This positive pressure got them doing the right thing. If they did it long enough, they discovered something: the brilliant insight that life is more fun to do right than it is to do wrong. They found out they wanted to keep doing the right thing. When young men and women finished high school in the youth home, they often didn't want to leave. They recognized the good pressure in the home was much better than the bad pressures they would face in the world.

I can guarantee that you won't be successful if you let godless people gain your ear. A famous football coach once said, "If you are gonna sleep in a sewer, you are gonna smell like a sewer." (Actually, he used a few different words that I didn't want to put in this book, but that's the gist of it.)

Here are four principles to remember regarding peer pressure.

1. Beware

Beware: every single person reading this book is capable of succumbing to peer pressure. All of us have moral shyness. When Israel went into the land of Canaan, God said, "I don't want any of the Canaanites left alive. They cannot live in the land with you. You must kill them all." Why would God order an ethnic cleansing? Because God recognized that the Canaanites' worship was immoral and that Israel would succumb to it. "[Israel] mingled with the nations and learned their practices, and served their idols, which became a snare to them" (Ps. 106:35–36).

Every one of us can succumb. This is not just an issue for young people. You can be silent in your job and let things happen that shouldn't because you're afraid to stand out as a believer. You can stand around and listen to someone gossip without saying anything because it is easier to go along. All of us can do it.

2. Distinguish between Patients and Friends

I always get the same question when I teach on this material. "Wait a minute, Tom. Didn't Jesus say a physician is not sent to the healthy but to the sick? Shouldn't I be trying to reach lost people?"

Of course you should. It is true that separation from sin is not isolation from sinful men. But you have to distinguish between your patients and your friends. If you are a follower of Christ, you are a physician. People who are dead in their sins are sick. And if we, as doctors, catch their disease, we won't be very useful as physicians.

We are entering into relationships with sinners to help them. Our attitude needs to be that people without Christ are off center. At first you may have a problem with that as it sounds kind of arrogant. But that's exactly the way God's Word instructs us to view the world. By God's grace, we believe the truth of the gospel. People outside the covenant are following an error and are lost and will perish. We need to think like Jesus: "You're sick. I'm healthy and I'm here to help you." If you have that attitude, you can surround yourself with all the wicked men you'd like, as long as you balance it with godly people who get close to you as advisors and comrades. But we are not here to learn all the things the Canaanites are doing.

As a pastor I minister to a lot of fallen people, and I make a distinction between my patients and my friends. The patients are not my friends—not in a true, deep, intimate way. I truly like them and want the best for them. But they don't get my ear. They don't get my heart. I don't live for their pleasure. You have to distinguish between the two.

Jude is the last exhortation of the New Testament before the book of Revelation. Jude's final words to the church that is being christened to go out into an ocean of evil: "Have mercy on some, who are doubting; save others, snatching them out of the fire; and on some have mercy with fear, hating even the garment polluted by the flesh" (Jude 1:22–23).

When you have people who are caught on the fence, unsure of the right way or the wrong way, be merciful to them and be kind to them. Go to them. Don't hide in your convent or monastery; go to those people, feel sorry for those hurting people.

There are also some people who are not doubting but are just caught up in this world and are being destroyed. Jude says, "Don't just sit there and watch these people burn." Reach your hand down there in the midst of them and get them out of there. You can do that.

But he also gives us a warning. Be afraid. Be very afraid. Even though you love them and have mercy on them and snatch them, you've also got to hate their wicked language, their wicked belief system, and their wicked activities.

You have to make sure you make a correct appraisal of their external sinful lives. Don't catch their disease and start believing the lies of this world. Jude says to mix it up but make sure you don't get sucked in. While you're in this wicked world, be careful. "Brethren, even if anyone is caught in any trespass, you who are spiritual, restore such a one in a spirit of gentleness; each one looking to yourself, so that you too will not be tempted" (Gal. 6:1).

3. Make Sure Who You Surround Yourself With

Be very selective as to who gets your ear and the innermost part of your heart. David said, "I am a companion of all those who fear You" (Ps. 119:63). Solomon said, "Iron sharpens iron, so one man sharpens another" (Prov. 27:17).

A piece of iron gets sharpened when it is rubbed the wrong way. Make sure you're surrounded by people who will not just tolerate you but challenge you. Are those the people that you've let close to you? David had a man on his staff, Hushai the Archite, the king's friend (1 Chron. 27:33). He was a godly man who was devoted to David. Do you have a personal friend that will challenge you? David said, "My eyes shall be upon the faithful of the land, that they may dwell with me; he who walks in a blameless way is the one who will minister to me" (Ps. 101:6). David surrounded himself with people who made him better.

You know what I'd do if I were you? I would make sure that I cultivated a group of friends in a small group. Where do you find these friends? You are not going to just stumble into them. They're not that common. Acquaintances are a dime a dozen. People who will whisper nice platitudes in your ears are everywhere. But if you want to surround yourself with biblically successful people, you are going to have to work. If you or I wanted to take a picture of an eagle, we probably couldn't go walk around our neighborhood and find an eagle. We'd have to go to Colorado and then climb way up in the mountains because eagles build their nests at high altitudes. Now if you wanted to take a picture of some run-of-the-mill, brown, sorry-looking sparrow, just stick your head outside your door and you'll see them flying all over the place. Do you understand? If you want to climb a good live oak or an elm, you'll have to look around because those are excellent hardwoods. But if you want to fool around in some old hackberry or glorified shrub, just walk around outside because there is one on every corner.

The same thing is true about people. If you want some dead-wood friends, just start hanging out with whoever will take you. But if you want to find excellent friends, you will have to hustle. I'll tell you what I'd do; if your church has small groups, I would call the pastor or coordinator and say, "I would like to join a group of people who want to be great for God."

I spoke recently to a group in Lubbock, Texas. I had a fellow come up to me and say, "My brother-in-law and my sister are in your church, and I've gotta tell you: their lives have been utterly transformed."

I said, "Really, tell me about it," thinking I was about to get a little glory.

He said, "They love their small group. A few months ago they evaluated their lives and said they wanted to get out of their rut as mediocre Christians. Instead of getting in a group where you simply had to have a pulse, they wanted to get serious. So they found a group where they memorize Scripture, are held accountable for quiet times, for discipling others, for sharing their testimony. Now their lives have been transformed."

Now that's a smart couple, whoever they are. If I were you, I would do the same thing. If you don't make sure you've got some great people close to you, those places will be filled with mediocre people. Deliberately surround yourself with great men and great women.

4. Be Willing to Die

In this wicked world, if push comes to shove among your peers, you have to be willing to stand all by yourself. When everybody else bows—because they will at some point—you stand. Can you do that? Consider what Peter said: "For the time already past is sufficient for you to have carried out the desire of the Gentiles, having pursued a course of sensuality, lusts, drunkenness, carousing, drinking parties and abominable idolatries. In all this, they are surprised that you do not run with them into the same excesses of dissipation, and they malign you" (1 Pet. 4:3–4).

To put that in Tom Nelson's Texas Bible, it means, "You've had enough time to live wickedly; it's time to live righteously. Don't be thinking that you're not gonna catch some heat. Your sorry old buddies will be amazed that you lifted yourself up out of that mire and they won't like it. Your life will be a witness against them, and so they're gonna do their best to pull you back down."

David faced this. "The arrogant utterly deride me, yet I do not turn aside from Your law" (Ps. 119:51). "They almost destroyed me on earth, but as for me, I did not forsake Your precepts" (Ps. 119:87). "Even though princes sit and talk against me, Your servant meditates on Your statutes" (Ps. 119:23). David's mantra: I don't care what anybody else says against me; I follow God.

I once went out to Lubbock, Texas, to watch my son play baseball for the Kansas Jayhawks against Texas Tech University. College baseball is unlike any other sport. No other team sport played in this country lets a person on the field hear the people in the stands. At football games or basketball games, there's too much noise from the crowd—you can't hear an individual fan.

At college baseball games you can hear individual fans because it's quiet between pitches and there aren't enough people to drown out a loud voice. So one slightly inebriated underclassman can be heard on the whole field. About three thousand fans from Texas Tech were in the stands at the game I attended. Texas Tech has a great baseball program, but all their fans are bitter from having to live in West Texas. If you've ever been to West Texas, you understand. They roll out of bed in the morning mad. They look out the window at that flat wasteland and say, "Gosh, I hate life."

So these bitter people come to the game. Now what kind of person goes to an event where men are competing and then sits in the stands making fun of them? They're the guys who quit athletics after T-ball at the YMCA. After the game, these little spindly fellows are out in the parking lot, playing with a Hacky Sack. (Why am I writing like this? Partly because Texas Tech beat my boy's team three games in a row and also because I know my friends in West Texas will read this book.)

While we were watching our boys get whupped pretty good, the heckling was incessant. I'll begrudgingly admit it takes a certain degree of talent to be able to heckle with depth and thoroughness. If a player has any minor defect, they'll search the Internet to build a whole history in preparation for the game. There is a little guy on our team who is about five foot six, and the whole stands were calling him "Stumpy" the entire game. "Stumpy, watch out for a divot; you're gonna fall in it."

It's hard to play when you're warming up with people screaming insults from thirty feet away. It's also not easy to be a fan of the other team. The Kansas fans had their own section—all thirty of us. We were so outnumbered, it was easy to be self-conscious. Here you are with a Kansas shirt in the middle of this sea of red and black. I had to have a hat, so I brought a generic hat. I wasn't about to wear a Kansas Jayhawk hat sitting out in the middle of those fans.

There was a notable exception among the Kansas fans: two little boys, Matt, nine, and Miles, six, at the game. They were sitting there with Kansas shirts and Kansas hats. They painted their faces blue and red and put a big "KU" on the cheek. At one point I looked down and Matt was gone. I asked his mom where he was, and she said, "He went to get a Coke."

"Alone?" I said, alarmed. "Dressed like that?"

These boys weren't even native Kansas fans. They are from Gruver, Texas. Do you know why they were at the game, cheering like maniacs for Kansas in a sea of Texas Tech fans? Because my son, John Clark Nelson, had come to Gruver, Texas, and gone by their house and played ball with them. He bent down to them and autographed a ball for them. He was their buddy. That's why they were at that game.

Do you think these boys were self-conscious? Do you think they were pressured by three thousand fans rooting against them? They didn't care if those other fans didn't like them. Why? Because John Clark came and bent down and learned their names and played ball with them. They love him. They didn't see the crowd. They had their eyes on one man.

That's the way we need to be in life. Wear Christ boldly. He has come down and done for us what no one else would or could do. People don't like it? Tough! They don't love us. They don't die for us. They don't come down to where we are. They don't know our names. So, I don't care what anybody thinks. We bear His name, and we wear His colors to honor the One who gave His life for us and lives now to love us and intercede for us at the right hand of God (Rom. 8:34).

You cannot be successful in life when you surround yourself with people who are not. You cannot be successful unless you surround yourself with great people. You cannot be successful unless you are willing to stand up for the One who died for you. Make sure you know the difference between those you minister to and those who minister to you.

Biblical success comes when you

1. surround yourself with people who can help you be successful,
2. beware of putting yourself in a situation that will make provision for the flesh (i.e., "tempt you").
3. distinguish between patients and friends,
4. cultivate lasting friendships with people who help you become more godly,
5. wear Christ boldly and be willing to die.

A PRAYER FOR TRUE SUCCESS

Father, give us a heart for one gaze, one face, one set of eyes, one approval—Yours. Grant us the courage to find real friends and to not be seduced by those who bring us down. Let us have mercy on those who are doubting, as we save others, snatching them out of the fire. But let us hate the garment that is corrupted by their flesh. We want to bind ourselves to Your people for Your glory. We ask this in Jesus' name. Amen.

THINKING MORE DEEPLY ABOUT TRUE SUCCESS

1. Can you remember a time when you experienced peer pressure? What was the situation? How did you respond?

2. Has it been difficult for you to find people who can offer positive peer pressure? Why or why not?

3. Have you ever had to "distinguish between patients and friends"? What was the situation? What happens if you get the two confused?

4. Can you remember a time when you were ridiculed for standing up for Christ? Can you remember a time when you denied Christ to avoid persecution? What does it take for us to become willing to die for Christ?

CHAPTER 9

The Workplace:

The Sacredness of the Secular

Aesop told a fable about a man who knew he was going to die and so he prepared his will. After he died, his sons read it. The will said that the man had a great treasure buried in his garden, and if his sons would dig for it, they would find it. Well, the sons went out and they dug, but they couldn't find it. So they moved to another location in the garden and dug some more. They continued to dig and dig and dig but never discovered any treasure.

However, all of their digging in that garden loosened the soil so much that the next year they had an incredible bumper crop. The moral of the story is, where there is great work, there is great treasure. Your digging and sweating in this garden can yield great, though unexpected, treasure.

You probably know a man who had a job that wasn't a perfect fit, so he left it for another. And this wasn't the first time. His search upsets his family and creates incredible instability because he cannot deal with problems in the workplace.

Another woman wants money quickly; she just doesn't want to work. So she tries stuff she should avoid in an attempt to get rich quick. Another man wants to make money but doesn't want to spend any time or money to do it. So he cuts the quality of his work and turns out shoddy products. Or he cheats and loses his integrity and his good name.

Another person works hard but can't get along with the boss; she can't deal with authority and keeps getting fired. As a result, her life is in a constant state of tumult.

Do you know those people? I've certainly seen them come and go.

You cannot be successful in life when you are a failure in the institution where you spend more than half of your waking days—the workplace. Sadly enough, our work often defines who we are. It shouldn't, but it does. Therefore, you can't be happy in life and a failure at work.

So we need to add one more item to our list of attributes of a biblically successful person:

a foundation of fearing God and gathering wisdom
the ability to maintain relationships
values
integrity
self-control
submission to authority
shock absorbers to deal with difficult times
positive peer pressure
a correct view of work

Finding Success at Work

How do you find true success in your work? Work for the glory of God. "Fine," you say, "I've heard that. But what do I do tomorrow at 8:00 a.m. when the chaos starts and the pressure begins to build?" Simply understand and apply what the Bible says about work and success.

Work is a good thing. As a matter of fact, work is a divine thing. God works. "He rested on the seventh day from all His work" (Gen. 2:2). In Genesis 1 and 2, Adam and Eve are told to work and cultivate the garden. Sin doesn't come into the world until Genesis 3, so even in the blissful state of Eden, Adam and Eve were supposed to work.

Jesus Christ works in and through the church. We are called His workmanship. The Bible commands us to work. The apostle Paul said, "If anyone is not willing to work, then he is not to eat, either" (2 Thess. 3:10). He also said, "He who steals must steal no longer; but rather he must labor, performing with his own hands what is good, so that he will have something to share with one who has need" (Eph. 4:28).

We were made for work. Part of the image of God in us is the desire to create and produce. That's why work can be so fulfilling and exciting—it touches a part of us that is deeply divine.

At the same time, work is also flawed. The earth does not yield itself to us like it did before the Fall. We no longer work in a perfect world. Work is hard because the world and its people are not the way they were meant to be. Work has become a minefield of potential broken relationships, materialistic temptations, prideful ambitions, and poor ethical decisions. Work can still be a blessing, but too often it becomes a curse.

We need biblical wisdom to truly succeed in our workplace. Here are seven core truths that can make work a blessing and not a curse.

1. Work in Reverence

The first truth is that all our work should be done in an attitude of reverence and love for God. "But you shall remember the Lord your God, for it is He who is giving you power to make wealth" (Deut. 8:18).

If you can do a task that people are willing to pay you for, God is the one who enables you to do it. God's grace gives you the ability to make wealth. As a matter of fact, Paul, writing to Timothy, said, "Instruct those who are rich in this present world not to be conceited or to fix their hope on the uncertainty of riches, but on God, who richly supplies us with all things to enjoy" (1 Tim. 6:17).

Your ability to work, to make money, and to enjoy it is God-given. But God doesn't give everybody the same gifts. Some of us have abilities that don't make much money. Some have great abilities to make lots of money, but that's OK. God doesn't have to give everyone the same skills, but He is just and He is good. So work reverently.

In Israel, keeping the Sabbath signified that you were working for God. You didn't just work six days and start over; you took a day to say "thank You" to God. The Sabbath is a day of worship to show that we realize that He gives us the ability to sustain our lives for another week.

After the first harvest of the year, God commanded Israel to shut everything down and have a party. It was a festival to God, who gave the early and late rains. The Israelites gave the sacrifice of a thank offering and a grain offering when they brought in their crops, saying "thank You" when good things happened. They had a free will or a concord offering, saying "thank You" to God for what He did for them. A tenth of everything they produced went to God, not because He needed it but because the people needed to acknowledge that He gave it to them.

When God gave the law to Moses, He said if the people forsook Him and worshipped the gods of nature He would turn off the spigot and make the heavens brass and the earth powder. He said He would curse them so that they would know He was the One who gave them the ability to make wealth.

So, in love, I'm going to tell you something straight. In any job that you do, don't get cocky because it's the grace of God that allows us to do anything. If you are a musician, it is the grace of God that gives you the ability to sing. If you are a mechanic, it's the grace of God that gives you the ability to turn a screw. If you are in finance, God gives you the brain power to be able to manage money. If one little artery in your head swelled and popped, your ability would be gone. Your ability to work could be gone faster than you can finish this sentence.

Work with reverence—it's the grace of God. Again, "it is He who is giving you power to make wealth" (Deut. 8:18).

2. Work Hard

The Bible is clear that success only comes through hard work. "By working hard in this manner you must help the weak" (Acts 20:35). "Whatever you do, do your work heartily, as for the Lord rather than for men" (Col. 3:23). "Like vinegar to the teeth and smoke to the eyes, so is the lazy one to those who send him" (Prov. 10:26).

Don't be lazy or make excuses. Don't be irresponsible—that's the work of a sluggard. It's the sluggard who doesn't finish. It's the sluggard who does sloppy work. Believers should work hard and take responsibility for their actions.

Mr. W. L. Brown is an eighty-five-year-old man in my church. As a young man in Chicago, he finished studying at a trade school in the middle of the Depression. He had a place to stay but didn't have anything to eat. He put on his best shirt and a tie, then went to the owner of a delicatessen and said, "Sir, I'm hungry, and I don't have any money or food. Can I do some work and then have something to eat?"

The man said, "Sure, son, you sit down and pull up a chair and eat and when you're finished I'll find you something to do." And W. L. said, "No, sir. I'll work first and then after I work, if I'm worth anything, you feed me." And so W. L. loosened his tie and put on an apron. He swept the floor, washed dishes, bussed tables, and cleaned up the kitchen for the man. When he was done, that man sat him down and fed him.

The store owner had never quite seen a kid like this. You know what he did? He tried to hire W. L. on the spot. Everybody wants to be associated with that rare person who has integrity and industry. He wanted him on his staff. Work hard.

3. Work As unto God

To repeat, Paul said, "Do your work heartily, as for the Lord rather than for men" (Col. 3:23). Paul wrote to the slaves on the island of Crete and told them to do their work "not pilfering, but showing all good faith so that they will adorn the doctrine of God our Savior in every respect" (Titus 2:10).

The word *adorn* in the Greek is the word *kosmeo*, which means "to add a cosmetic or to beautify." A hard worker beautifies his testimony by his labors.

Oscar Hammerstein was once asked about why he worked so hard to perfect his lyrics. He answered the questioner with a story about seeing a photo of the Statue of Liberty taken from a helicopter. He was amazed to see the sculptor's detail on Lady Liberty's hairdo because the statue was made in 1886—long before anyone thought of having the capability of flying overhead to check up on his work. Why would someone spend time working on the top of the head of a 180-foot statue? Because Frederic Bartholdi, the Frenchman who made it, knew that liberty was grand and glorious and he wasn't willing to do a halfhearted job.

And so Hammerstein realized that if Bartholdi could do his work with excellence for the concept of liberty, then he could do his music well for his audience. And so he strived for perfection and greatness in everything he did. There's an old saying that any culture that has great philosophy but bad plumbing in the next generation will have neither. Bad plumbers make for lousy philosophers. Do your work to the glory of God.

Four times a week I come to our church building at 6:00 a.m. to work with young men. When I finish and walk through the building, Dave Feree and Ed Havens are working on repairing and maintaining the building. They are often in early and stay late to keep the facilities in good shape.

I love to hear them working because they work to music. What music do you think these men work to? They play baroque organ pieces by Johann Sebastian Bach on the tape player and fill this building with the sounds of the composer who signed his work, "Sola Gloria Deo": "to the glory of God alone." I love to see these men vacuuming, fixing chairs, and hanging doors to the glory of God. That's the way it should be for all of us. Work to the glory of God.

When I speak of the Shakers—the religious group—what do you immediately think of? Shaker furniture. Why do you think of Shaker furniture? Because that's what they're known for. It's the best, simplest, starkest, most durable furniture you can find. Do you know who the Shakers really are? They are one of the most oblique, weird, obtuse cults in the history of Christianity. They were started by a woman in England named Ann Lee who believed she was the incarnation of the female aspect of God. To be part of this cult you had to treat her words as emanations from God. You did not marry because marriage and sexuality were evil. Members of the cult walked in a particular way around a circle with their hands held up until the spirit fell on them and then they shook as they encountered God. That's why they were called Shakers.

It's a strange group of folks. So why when I say Shakers, why didn't you think of the strangest variance of orthodoxy in history? Because they have one point of their religion that is orthodox—they believe that "work is worship." Anything that their hands did had to be done to the glory of God. And so when they made a chair, it had to be a chair that God would be proud to say, "That's a chair that my kid made." Because they did their work as unto God, their furniture is famous throughout the world. Work as unto God.

4. Work As If Your Efforts Were Rewarded by God

The apostle Paul said to do your work unto the Lord, "knowing that from the Lord you will receive the reward of the inheritance" (Col. 3:24).

He wrote to slaves, instructing them to work not as unto men but to God because God rewards them for their work, "knowing that whatever good thing each one does, this he will receive back from the Lord, whether slave or free" (Eph. 6:8).

You might be asking, "Are you saying that part of our reward at the judgment seat of Christ will be based on how I vacuum?" Yes, I am. You and I are not rewarded simply because we do "religious" activities like prayer, giving, and preaching. We will be rewarded for living all of our lives to the glory of God. Work as though you are going to be called to account because you will.

5. Work Loyally

Paul put it this way: "Be obedient to those who are your masters according to the flesh, with fear and trembling, in the sincerity of your heart, as to Christ; not by way of eyeservice, as men-pleasers, but as slaves of Christ, doing the will of God from the heart. With good will render service, as to the Lord, and not to men" (Eph. 6:5–7).

Be loyal. If your boss is hard to get along with, talk to him. If you get fired, then get fired. If your boss is crooked, quit and do not be a part of a crooked institution. But if you're not going to talk to him and if you are not going to quit, don't slander him. If you're going to take from him the result of his labors, don't go behind his back. Even though you may think he is not treating you fairly, he doesn't owe you a job. If you can't confront him and you can't quit, don't create division by being disloyal.

Don't be like Absalom who stood at the gate and said (in the Tommy Nelson Translation), "You want justice? There is no justice in the land. Why, if I were king, there would be justice" (2 Sam. 15:4).

He sowed seeds of dissent and won the hearts of Israel away from the king, created a division, and started a civil war. What happened to Absalom? God killed him. One of the qualities of an ungodly leader in the book of Jude is divisiveness (Jude 1:19). They are grumblers who flatter for the sake of gaining an advantage. That's the quality of a perverse man. Don't sit around at that water fountain and talk about your sorry boss. Quit, confront him, or work loyally.

6. Work Honestly

The book of Amos condemns wicked business practices in the northern part of Israel. "Hear this, you who trample the needy, to do away with the humble of the land, saying, 'When will the new moon be over, so that we may sell grain, and the sabbath, that we may open the wheat market, to make the bushel smaller and the shekel bigger, and to cheat with dishonest scales, so as to buy the helpless for money and the needy for a pair of sandals, and that we may sell the refuse of the wheat?'" (Amos 8:4–6).

A shekel was a measure of weight. The seller put his weight on the scale, and the buyer had to put enough gold or silver on the scales to balance it. If the seller made the shekel bigger, he could cheat the buyer out of more of his money. "A false balance is an abomination to the Lord, but a just weight is His delight" (Prov. 11:1).

They would also make the bushel smaller. So when someone paid two shekels for a bushel of wheat, they received less wheat than they really purchased. God says that is an abomination as well.

The word *abomination* is also used for idolatry, perversion, bestiality, adultery, and murder. God said a false businessman is in the same class. The people trusted them and they violated their trust. God said that it's an abomination when a man trusts you and you cheat him.

God judged the northern kingdom for their dishonesty in their work. They practiced false advertising. They were deceitful.

You can be dishonest in your work in other ways. The book of James says, "Behold, the pay of the laborers who mowed your fields, and which has been withheld by you, cries out against you; and the outcry of those who did the harvesting has reached the ears of the Lord of Sabaoth. You have lived luxuriously on the earth and led a life of wanton pleasure; you have fattened your hearts in a day of slaughter" (James 5:4–5).

Not paying a person what he's worth is an abomination to God. God considered it so vile to put a person to work and not pay him that He says He will personally judge that land.

You can also be dishonest as a worker. The book of Titus says to workers, "Urge bondslaves to be subject to their own masters in everything, to be well-pleasing, not argumentative, not pilfering" (Titus 2:9–10).

Do you have anything in a desk drawer at home that shouldn't be there? Don't steal! The elders of our church are all businessmen. Recently in a meeting, we were talking about honesty. To a man, they told me that employee theft is a major problem in each of their companies. Many major corporations actually have a line in their budget for employee theft. In most stores today the video cameras are not just focusing on the shoppers, but also on the employees.

I can say before God that I have never, ever stolen anything from a store. Do you know why? Because my mama would have killed me. She would have put me down like Old Yeller—"boom!"—right there in the yard. She would have told the neighbors, "We had four boys. Now we only have three. We killed little Tommy. He was a thief."

There's nobody sorrier than a thief who takes things that someone else earned and made. When you are a thief, you not only violate one of the commandments of God, you violate the dignity of man. You violate your name, and the image of God within you.

We have had people steal from our church. We don't pass an offering plate; we use boxes at the back of the auditorium where people drop their contributions. Several times we have had people steal from those boxes. One guy would come to our church, sit through the service, wait until everybody had left, and then steal from the giving boxes.

That sounds extreme. I'm sure you are saying to yourself, "I'd never do anything like that." But all of us are tempted to be less than honest in small ways. We shift the blame to others when something isn't finished or doesn't work out well. We take additional credit when things are a success. We round up on expense accounts or time sheets, justifying it by saying that the company owes me for all I have done. We surf the Internet during work hours or make personal phone calls or spend too much time shooting the breeze with a coworker.

In Genesis, Jacob is able to say to his dishonest uncle, Laban, "My honesty will answer for me later" (Gen. 30:33). Are you scrupulously honest? If not, you cannot find true success in your work.

7. Work with Excellence

"Do you see a man skilled in his work? He will stand before kings; He will not stand before obscure men" (Prov. 22:29). Every one in business is on the lookout for excellence. Do your work rightly, and men will almost always take notice. But even if they don't, God will.

It is said that Leonardo da Vinci was working on a painting with his apprentice. The student was amazed at the beauty of the work Leonardo was doing. One day, da Vinci handed his student the brush and said, "Finish the painting." The young man drew back in horror at the thought. Da Vinci exclaimed, "Have not I myself inspired you? Finish!"

Da Vinci believed that his inspiration would be enough to help the young man paint with excellence. In the same way, seeing the glory of God inspires us to excellence. Look around you at the amazing work God does every day; you'll be inspired to do your work right.

Ben Jonson wrote about this in his poem, "The Noble Nature."

> It is not growing like a tree
> In bulk, doth make Man better be;
> Or standing long an oak, three hundred year,
> To fall a log at last, dry, bald, and sere:
> A lily of a day
> Is fairer far in May,
> Although it fall and die that night—
> It was the plant and flower of Light
> In small proportions we just beauties see;
> And in short measures life may perfect be.

Jonson is saying that you don't have to be a majestic three-hundred-year-old oak to be beautiful. Even a huge oak shall some day collapse and die into nothing but a bald, dried log. Even though the lily was something that died after a day, it was still the child of light. It was still God's creation.

They are real beauties, both of them. Whether it's a majestic oak or a little bitty lily, they are still lovely. In short measures, life, in the same way, may perfect be. You don't have to be Michelangelo painting the Sistine Chapel to glorify God. You don't have to be Christopher Wren building the great buildings of London to glorify God. You can glorify God in the simplicity of your job if it is done with greatness.

Not everyone will be a president or CEO. Not everyone will win the sales contests or get the big promotion. Not everyone will start their own business, manage an office, or become a master craftsman. But that doesn't mean your work is not important. It also doesn't mean your work shouldn't glorify God through its excellence. Edgar Guest said it this way in his poem, "Results and Roses":

> The man who wants a garden fair,
> Or small, or very big,
> With flowers growing here and there
> Must bend his back and dig.
> The things are mighty few on earth
> That wishes can attain.
> Whate'er we want of any worth
> We've got to work to gain.
> It matters not what goal you seek,
> Its secret here reposes:
> You've got to dig from week to week
> To get results or roses.

Whether you are striving for a great life or growing roses, you've got to sweat and work honestly and excellently.

No Work Required

Now let me add this important caveat: In one area of life God asks you to do nothing. As a matter of fact, if you try to make it happen on your own, you will fail in the worst way.

God doesn't want you to try to save yourself or make yourself good enough to have a right relationship with Him. You can try to make your life presentable to God, inducing Him to count you righteous and take you to heaven, but it won't work. He doesn't need it. It's an insult to do it. He has already decreed that you are saved by Jesus' work and not your own.

So work excellently in your job. Work excellently with whatever you do, but as far as salvation, the Bible says (see Eph. 2:8–9), it is not by works, don't try it. Rather, God has done it for you.

The perfect life that you couldn't live has already been lived for you by God becoming a man and living it in your place. And the atonement for your iniquity, that you cannot pay for, He has already paid for.

This is the workmanship of God. He has created this masterpiece called salvation. On this work He will not let you assist Him; He'll not let you help. He will not let you hold one nail in your hand. Jesus did it all: "This is My beloved Son, in whom I am well-pleased" (Matt. 3:17). But as for us, "all have sinned and fall short of the glory of God" (Rom. 3:23).

Isn't that good news? It's done. You don't have to do it. You might be thinking, *Tom, that's too easy! Surely there must be more to becoming a Christian than that?* Easy for whom? It was not easy for Jesus Christ to hang on that cross with the nails piercing His body. Your job is to accept this salvation that comes by God's grace.

After you have that salvation, then by faith and out of love for God, labor to glorify Him. If you're a mechanic, work fairly and with excellence. If you're a teacher, instruct well. If no one else cares, you do it simply because of the eyes of God the Father that see you as His child.

Chuck Swindoll tells the story of how he pulled into a service station once to get his oil changed. The attendant rolled under his car, detached the pan, and cleaned it. As the attendant was fastening the piece back on the car, Chuck said, "Why'd you clean that part that nobody is ever going to see?" The mechanic said, "Because I see it! My work is who I am and I do it right." Chuck knew where he was going to take his car from then on.

How do you find an honest mechanic? We all know there are many honest mechanics out there, but we also know there are many shops that make money selling unnecessary services to car owners.

Dr. Haddon Robinson told the story of one of these investigations in Toronto a number of years ago. A writer for a local paper took a spark-plug wire off of his engine, making the car run unevenly. He took the car in to different shops and asked them to fix it. Time after time people sold him unnecessary repairs or charged him for repairs that were not done.

Finally, he went to a small garage. A fellow named Fred came out, popped open the hood, and said, "Let me listen to that thing." After a few seconds, he told the reporter, "I think I know what's wrong." He reached down and grabbed the wire, announcing, "Your spark-plug wire came off." And he put it back.

The reporter said, "What do I owe you?"

"I'm not gonna charge you anything," Fred replied. "I didn't have to fix anything; I just reattached the wire."

The writer then told him what he was doing and that he had been charged all kinds of money by mechanics looking at that same wire. He asked Fred, "Why didn't you charge me anything?"

Fred said, "Are you sure you want to know? I happen to be a Christian and believe that everything we do should be done to glorify Him. I'm not a preacher and I'm not a missionary, but I am a mechanic and so I do it honestly. I do it skillfully and I do it to the glory of God."

The next day in the newspaper was a headline that read, "Christian Mechanic, Honest to the Glory of God."

I would dare say that all of the preachers and pastors and missionaries in Canada that day did not have any greater effect for the kingdom of God and for the glory of God as that one honest mechanic.

"Whatever you do, do your work heartily, as for the Lord rather than for men."

Biblical success comes when you

1. understand that work is one of the ways we reflect the image of God,
2. work in an attitude of reverence and love for God,
3. work hard,
4. work for the glory of God,
5. work to be rewarded by God,
6. are loyal in your work,
7. are honest as an employer and employee,
8. work with excellence.

A Prayer for True Success

Father, give us the right perspective on our work—from the smallest task to the largest project. The Milky Way galaxy is no larger in Your gaze than the rug that we vacuum. Poor work besmirches our testimony and stains Your name. We pray that our work would be honoring, worshipful, and excellent. Help us see our work as holy in Your sight. We ask this in Jesus' name. Amen.

Thinking More Deeply about True Success

1. What is one of your most frustrating experiences with work? Why was it difficult? What did you learn?
2. Work is both a blessing and a curse after the Fall. How has this been true for you? What biblical truths help you deal with this dual nature of work?

3. What is the purpose of a Sabbath? Do you celebrate a Sabbath regularly in your life? Why or why not? What difference do you think this could make?

4. Is it easy for you to work while remembering that your efforts will be rewarded by God? Why or why not?

CHAPTER 10

Marriage:

Foundation for Joy or Rock in Your Shoe?

Biblical success is not a sprint; it's a marathon. Sometimes we get impatient, wanting to hit the home run that will get us to the final destination of success. But the reality is that success comes by hitting singles over and over again. The road to true success starts when you are born and ends when you take your last breath. Having long-term, godly success requires faithfulness.

If you've ever jogged for exercise, you know that if you were to start a marathon and then notice a rock in your shoe after the first couple of steps, you wouldn't keep running. Even though that rock may be a little irritation right now, by mile ten you'll start noticing it at every step. At about mile fifteen, you'll be dreading every time your foot hits the ground. And by mile twenty, you'll try to be the first person to finish a marathon hopping on one foot.

Your shoes are not merely elements of your race; they are the foundation on which you stand. If you have a rock in your shoe at the beginning of a marathon, you have to stop right there and make it right. You can't afford to take another step until you take off that shoe and get the rock out. Then you can proceed and finish the race.

Having a godly marriage is as integral to a life of success as good shoes are to a marathon. You better get marriage right at the start; if you don't, it will come back to haunt you. If you are not married, read this chapter as preparation for the time when God might bring someone into your life. If you are divorced, read this chapter as part of your healing process. Remember that God forgives and restores—that's the very heart of the gospel.

Our list of attributes of a biblically successful person would not be complete without adding to it the idea of a successful marriage:

a foundation of fearing God and gathering wisdom
the ability to maintain relationships
values
integrity
self-control
submission to authority
shock absorbers to deal with difficult times
positive peer pressure
a correct view of work
a biblically healthy marriage

The Long Consequence of a Bad Marriage

I hear the stories over and over again. An intelligent and gifted young man goes to school, does well, and graduates. He's ambitious, gets a good job in a firm, starts his career. Life looks rosy. He meets a girl, falls in love, they get married. Unfortunately, a lot of those virtues he had—the determination, focus, and ambition—also mean that he can be inflexible. He's always right. He can be intolerant. He can be so focused that he's a bad listener.

She saw him as a rock, but there are some worms under "the rock." His wife comes to him and begins to talk about the alienation she feels. He basically tells her to get over it. They have a couple of kids, who are raised in this eggshell-type environment—always careful about everything they say or do around Dad. They can't wait until they are sixteen to get a driver's license, so they can leave the house. The daughter can't wait to get some other man's arms around her because her father didn't know how to love.

He'd been taught how to make a living, but nobody taught him how to live. Pretty soon, there is infidelity and then there is a divorce. But he doesn't want to live alone, so another family is blended into the mix. By the time this guy is in his mid-forties, what started out as a rock in his shoe is now consuming his entire leg. This marriage that he considered a neat addition to his life has now cancelled out all the happiness of his accomplishments. What God provided to be a source of joy has become a source of daily frustration and heartache.

His ex-wife was a very talented, sharp, ambitious girl in college, but now she is so hurt that she can't communicate. She withdraws into the despair of a woman whose self-esteem has been crushed. She starts looking for someone who will love her and treat her with kindness. She is vulnerable and lonely.

Does this sound familiar? After twenty-five years of pastoring, I could put a thousand names to that scenario. And I could give you five other scenarios that would fit thousands more.

You cannot be happy and successful in life when your marriage is in shambles. Your marriage is not simply something you add on to the side of your life; it is something you are. You truly have become one flesh. Marriage is inseparable from your very life. And great marriages are an exclusive club—only the selfless can be members.

Sometimes I think many people should be categorically disqualified from ever being married. But out of an innate desire not to be lonely, they get married. And they end up cursing their lives.

In this chapter, we'll cover four foundational beliefs for true success in marriage. And then I'll offer you seven foundational actions. Belief and behavior—four things you need to believe, seven acts of behavior. These are not optional—you don't get to pick your favorite eight out of eleven. If you miss one of these, your marriage will eventually have serious problems, as will your life.

We will all struggle with these, but I hope to struggle long and well. That's what makes a good marriage instead of a bad one; the willingness to struggle.

Belief 1: Fear of God

We covered the fear of God at the beginning of this book, so now I want to show you how this applies in marriage. The fear of God means that you do the right things for the right reasons. I used to be confused when I read that verse that says, "If anyone comes to Me, and does not hate his own father and mother and wife and children and brothers and sisters, yes, and even his own life, he cannot be My disciple" (Luke 14:26). It doesn't look like it makes a lot of sense. "You have to love Me more than these people to be My disciple." And then as I progressed in the Christian life, I realized that was the most wonderful notion you could have. When you love God supremely, then your faith determines your actions. You will be doing the right things for the right reason. You will be consistent.

For instance, I spoke in San Antonio this week. I didn't know what my wife was doing for two days, but that doesn't bother me. I'll tell you why. Because I know who my wife is and I know who my wife fears and I know who my wife loves.

It's not that I know my wife will act a certain way. I know why she acts the way she acts, and it's not because of me. Otherwise, her actions would shift according to my faithfulness. She acts a certain way because of the un-movability of God.

You can't have a marriage if you don't have an immovable reason as to why you will be gentle, loving, faithful, kind, and respectful. In the creation it was God and Adam first, then Adam and Eve. God has to be central between two people before you can bring them together. You can do all the counseling and all the psychological and philosophical talking about relationships that you want, but it's not worth a hill of beans if you're not trusting in something that doesn't move. And the only thing we have that doesn't move is God. So the first foundational belief for marriage is that both individuals must fear God and seek to obey Him. Good behavior has its roots and life in the fear of God.

Belief 2: Roles

A number of years ago, Pierre Mornell, a secular counselor, wrote a book after thirty-eight years of counseling. *Passive Men, Wild Women* summarized the frustrations of women who were tired and discouraged. They were tired of seeing men be creative, active, initiating, and spontaneous on the job and then totally passive in the home. If either the husband or the wife shirks their responsibilities, you will have a disastrous marriage.

This is not a popular subject, but the farther we stray from biblical truth, the more of a mess we make in our society. Both the husband and wife have dogmatic commands from God as to who they are to be and what they are to do within marriage. In every environment—whether on the job, in a game, or in a home—everyone needs to know their roles before you start.

As to marriage, God has spoken very clearly. Adam is created first and then Eve. Adam is called the head. Eve is called the body. Husbands are called the head of their wives as Christ is to the church; and wives are called to submit, to willingly place themselves underneath the wing of their husbands. Husbands lead; wives have input, give opinions, or lovingly challenge, but wives follow. You can't have two masters, and God has said that males lead.

After working with men and women for twenty-five years, all the notions of the radical feminists don't wash. Every woman who has a passive, lackadaisical husband is frustrated. Gloria Steinem said, "Some of us are becoming the men we wanted to marry."

If you are a woman reading this book, give me a minute before you throw it in the fireplace. How is a man supposed to lead biblically? He should love his wife like Christ loved the church. The way to lead is to die. A man should daily give up his life for this woman that God has so graciously given him.

That's the way you lead. This leadership ladder is shaped like a crucifix. If you will climb that cross, then you may willingly be over your wife. In all my years I have known very few women who had a problem submitting to a man on a cross.

Those are the rules. If you're a man, you might be saying, "Tom, can we reverse those, please? How about if I let her run things and I'll be submissive." No, God's edicts fit perfectly with the constitution of men and women. The male should sacrificially lead and the woman should be respectful.

Men need to lead. You're the protector of your home. You need to get up on Sunday and say, "Let's go, folks; let's get rolling." Go to your church, sing loud, off-key if you will, but sing loud. Don't just sit there like some inert lump; be a leader who is willing to die.

Belief 3: Responsibilities

There must be order in the home. Somebody has to have the weight on them for going out and performing a task, making the money, bringing it in to buy the food and the clothes and the goods to take care of things. God has said whose responsibility it is. Adam, you work by the sweat of your brow. Ladies, if you have a particular job that you want to do and you can juggle the home and the office, go right ahead, providing that you don't get too beat up by the extra workload. But the responsibility to provide is not the wife's. If she wants to help out in a tough situation, then that's her prerogative. But the responsibility of the food on that table is the husband's. That may sound old-fashioned, but that's OK because the Bible was written a long time ago.

There's nothing more frustrating to a woman than to be married to an irresponsible man who won't get off the dole. A long time ago, a woman in our church was married to a man who always wanted to make a million dollars, but he didn't want to work. Unless he had the ideal situation, he would not work, and she constantly had to bear the brunt of the responsibility. She finally left him. Although my thought was, *You know you shouldn't have done that*, I'll be real honest with you; I stand convicted, I didn't step in there. He put her in a situation that—even though she might have been wrong—certainly drove her toward that decision. And it sure seemed he deserved it because he was shiftless and lazy. Women know deep inside they were not made to be married to irresponsible, shiftless men.

Someone also has to have the responsibility for organizing and taking care of the home. In the Greek of the New Testament, the wife is called the *oikodespotes*, the "house despot" or ruler of the house. Women have the special privilege of bearing children and managing the home. Gentlemen, you still need to clean up after yourselves. It's a wonderful thing that I highly recommend. I try not to be overly proud of this, but I happen to be one of the greatest dish loaders in history. I'm a dish-loading fool. I can vacuum. I can make a bed. I do whatever I can to help my wife. However, we both understand the final responsibility for managing the home rests with her.

I came in yesterday from a trip and discovered she had taken my office and completely rearranged it, making it the most lovely-looking office. When I was there, it was a sty. She moved some furniture and did wonders. It was like June Cleaver got in my home for a little bit. It was wonderful.

It is frustrating to a husband when there is no order in the home. The wife should make sure that the home is managed. The men have to go out in the world and struggle. The women have to struggle in the home. Both of you should be sensitive and help each other out as much as you can.

Belief 4: Commitment

Even though you struggle, even though you quarrel, and even though at times you make each other cry, there has to be an underlying and undying commitment to one another. Divorce can never be mentioned in your home. Don't use it as a threat against your spouse. Unless someone is getting abused physically or unless someone is unfaithful, divorce is not an option. You will cause tremendous structural damage to your marriage and to your kids if you let that word be batted about.

I grew up in a wonderful, "Leave-It-to-Beaver" kind of home. But I remember my mother and father having an argument one time. They raised their voices at one another, and I didn't know what to think. I went to my mother and talked about it with her. She leaned close to me and said, "Your father and I might have arguments, and we might even get loud, but you never have to worry about us being together. We're here for the duration." I still remember that to this day. My house was solid.

If you have ever used the word *divorce* as a threat, veiled or otherwise, stop reading this book right now and go beg your spouse's forgiveness. You have to see it through. Divorce is not an option.

Commitment doesn't mean that you have to suck it up and be miserable until you die—that's not biblical commitment. Commitment says, "I'm going to flex and change. I'll apologize till Christ comes, but I will make sure this home stays peaceful." That's commitment!

These foundational beliefs are the north, east, south, west; they are what the structure of a godly marriage rests on. The fear of God, an understanding of roles, following through on responsibilities, and an undying commitment—are these present in your marriage? If not, pray and ask God to change your heart and mind.

On top of the foundation of these four beliefs, biblical success in marriage comes through seven actions. Let's look at them.

Action 1: Courtesy

Courtesy draws out a response of kindness. When you are courteous, a great marriage will follow. When you are discourteous, I don't care how wonderful you try to be, every other thing you do in marriage will be seen as hypocrisy. Do you know that?

One woman said to me, "At this point I don't really care if my husband is romantic. I just want him to be civil." Be careful to be courteous in how you speak to your mate, how you listen to them, how you refer to them, or how you touch them. If you're discourteous, a love note will be viewed with contempt and great, passionate sexuality will come across as manipulation. If you are discourteous, bringing home money to take care of your wife is seen as superficial atonement.

Courtesy means that you treat them in a courtly way. Men treat woman gently—as a vessel made of china, porcelain, or crystal.

Have you ever gone out in public with a couple who is discourteous in how they speak to each other? It's embarrassing, isn't it? Have you ever been out with a couple who is very kind in how they speak and listen and touch and refer? It is so edifying and uplifting.

If you are not careful, you can begin to take each other for granted and start going through the motions. We forget to soften our words and actions with kindness. We can just get into habits of discourtesy.

I am so glad Teresa and I began early on with a godly intolerance of discourtesy. So whenever I am harsh with her, she has a way of letting me know. She'll say, with her voiced pitched just the right way, "Was that rude?" Pause. "I think it was." That's when I know I better step back and get my heart right and show her some courtesy.

And then there are times that I will say to her, "Teresa, what did you just say? Was that critical? It sounded critical."

"Oh, no. It wasn't critical."

"OK, that's good, 'cause I thought it was critical."

And so we have a way of keeping each other smooth. It's sort of like trimming your big toenails so you won't stab your mate. There needs to be a holy discontent with discourtesy in your union.

If I introduced you to a famous person, like George W. Bush, what would you do? You'd offer him your hand and look him in the eyes and treat him as a dignitary. Yet within about fifteen seconds, he'll forget your name—just like you would forget his if the roles were reversed. So why would we treat him with such courtesy, and yet treat our spouse with discourtesy? She's the woman who has gone through labor for us. He's the man who goes out in the pit every day for us. Practice the discipline of courtesy.

Action 2: Esteem Your Spouse

We show our spouses that we value them. Esteem is how we communicate to people their distinctive worth, how wonderful they are. The woman in the Song of Solomon said, "I am the rose of Sharon, the lily of the valleys" (Song of Sol. 2:1). The lily and the rose are flowers of singular beauty. That's how her betrothed treated her. She said to him, "My beloved is to me a pouch of myrrh which lies all night between my breasts" (Song of Sol. 1:13).

To her, he was like perfume that she would wear around her neck, his memory close to her heart all night. That's the way we need to treat each other in marriage.

Charles Spurgeon, the great preacher of London, referred to his wife as "Sweety." She referred to him as "Tirshatha," which is a Hebrew word in the book of Nehemiah for "governor." (I said to my wife, "I like that: 'governor' has a nice ring to it.") Treat your spouse biblically, like you treat your own body.

Men should nourish and cherish their wives, like Christ treats His church. Treat her like a king would treat his crown. When I see a man disrespect his wife, I don't care how smart or how successful he is, he has fallen way down in my sight. If a man makes minimum wage and treats his wife with dignity, he has integrity and is worthy of respect.

The same thing is true for a woman. I feel embarrassed when I hear a woman deride her husband in public. It's embarrassing, degrading, and inappropriate. There is nothing a man wants more from his wife than respect. "Wives, be subject to your own husbands, as to the Lord. . . . Husbands, love your wives, just as Christ also loved the church and gave Himself up for her" (Eph. 5:22, 25).

Sometimes when men read this, they think of Christ's torture, execution, and death. They get ready to die in some terrible way for their wives. The reality is that there probably won't be a time in most men's lives when somebody says, "It's you or your wife." Rather than being so chivalrous on your dying day, how about being kind and considerate every day? Instead of dying for your wife, why don't you die to yourself and be kind and tender to your wife? Die for her one hour at a time.

Action 3: Communicate

In any relationship, you have to talk and you have to listen. We have to talk sweetly and deeply and easily and often. And then we have to listen carefully to truly hear what our partner is saying.

You need more than Level 1 communication. Level 1 communication acknowledges that the other person exists. "How are you doing?" "Pretty good." "Have a nice day." It's the way you're spoken to when you pick up a burger at Wendy's. That's fine for fast food, but you don't want to have a drive-through marriage.

Level 2 communication is the exchange of information, "How are you doing?" "Well, actually, I've got a little sinus drainage this morning." Level 3 communication shows concern about you as a person. "How are you doing?" "I have some sinus drainage." "I am sorry to hear that. You know what? Let's pray about it. God loves you. Give me a hug."

That's Level 3 communication and that is why people get married. It's why they fall in love. When they dated, they went to restaurants and sat across the table and looked into each other's eyes. There they talked of deep things and listened well. And they didn't hurt one another. They got close, and there was acceptance and celebration and bonding. And they said, "Man, I need forty more years of this." That's why we fall in love in the first place.

Unfortunately, that which was an instinct while you were dating has to become a discipline in marriage. It takes time to listen and to communicate. One practical idea for a married couple is to have couch time. Make time every day to sit down with your mate and face each other on the couch. When the kids come along, you say, "Scoot, scoot, scoot. Mom and Dad are talking here." Don't think you're going to psychologically damage your child; nothing could be more gratifying to your child to know the solidity of Mom and Dad's relationship.

Maybe you could use some drive time. Every once in awhile, Teresa and I'll say, "Let's go get a Dr Pepper over at Krum." We'll drive out to Krum, Texas, and we'll sit and talk. We'll listen to songs from the sixties and enjoy it, remembering when!

Perhaps you need to institute a date night. Wednesday night is our date night. Every Wednesday, I get to go to a quiet place and just enjoy being with Teresa. When I was young, I thought I would get to the place where I'd know her so completely we'd go through life staring blankly at each other. Now I realize she's like a spring; there are new things constantly coming up from within her that I want to know. Her experience of life filters through her and I love it. We have to communicate.

Like many men, this was hard for me. The area of communication was a place where I was weak. I had to learn to listen. There was a time when my wife grabbed my cheek and said, "Listen with your face." Just like that, she made me listen to her. I was a bad listener because I was trying to process information. We think we have the ability to watch ESPN, do the checkbook, and listen to our wives talk about their struggles all at the same time. "Um, that's tough . . . keep going . . . I'm here for you, baby, I'm here."

Women are interested in a lot more than just the exchange of information. Most of the time, they know the answer before they ever ask you the question. They want your face pointed at them just like Jesus' face is to you whenever you pray. To have a godly marriage, you have to communicate and listen.

Action 4: Spend Time with Each Other

When couples are dating, many of them want to reserve 6:00 p.m. until 2:00 a.m. every day to be together. And anything that threatens that time is seen as an inconvenience. If you've dated, you know what I am talking about. You went to a movie by yourselves. You ate together, talked together.

When you get married, it is different. Much of your time is spent doing all the things you have to do to keep a family going. You can become like two old mules yoked together. "Ah, there you are, Sally. Ready to start pulling? Better get going—we got about fifty years of this ahead of us."

The danger is that after a few job changes, illnesses, kids, operations, and cancer, you become like two Marines back to back. "It's your turn to take the kids." You just get tough, like old partners, who lean on each other. In one sense, that's OK. I always tell young couples, "Don't think marriage is a continual fount of effervescence and joy. A huge part of marriage is just being there for one another no matter how you feel."

But marriage is more than that. Marriage is also meant to include delight and intimacy and joy. Those aspects of our relationship are built when we spend time together. So every Wednesday night, my wife and I go out. And when I say "go out," I don't mean we run down to Wendy's. I mean I vacuum the car, brush my teeth, take her out, sit across from her and spend time together. Make it a priority, prepare for it, and treat it as an opportunity and a challenge. Guess what? Once you build the habit, it becomes fun and you'll never want to do without it. Your children will boast about your tenderness into the next generation.

Action 5: Fight Clean

All couples have conflict, so you need to learn to fight clean. When you have a conflict and you're the offended one, submission does not mean that you lay there and enable your mate to sin by hurting you. But it does mean that when you tell your spouse how you feel, you don't yell, call them names, and throw things. You don't slam the door and walk away. "A gentle answer turns away wrath, but a harsh word stirs up anger" (Prov. 15:1).

So you say, "Honey, what you said hurt me, it really did." Or you say, "Sugar, when you did that, I felt about two inches tall. That embarrassed me." If you're the offended one, talk gently. If you're the offender, don't turn away emotionally from your mate and say, "You'll just have to get over it."

I'm going to write this next sentence in all caps just to show you how important I believe this is. YOUR MARRIAGE WILL BE SAVED OR LOST RIGHT AT THIS POINT. Your mate does not assume that you're a perfect person. But they do hope that you can grow and improve. When you're mate says to you, "That hurt me," or "Honey, I'm lonely for you," or "Honey, I'm talking and you're not listening," don't give her some rationalistic syllogism. "Well, *A* leads to *B* and *B* leads to *C*, then *A* leads to *C*, and so you shouldn't feel that way." I can guarantee you she won't say, "Oh! OK, I feel good now!" Instead, she'll feel not only hurt, but ridiculed and hurt.

Don't sit with a smug smile on your face while she's talking. A buddy of mine used to do that before his wife hit him with a board. While she's talking, don't look at her and say, "Um hum, um hum, um hum, um hum." If you treat her like that, what do you think is her next step? She has shared her heart and you turn her away. She hurts, her heart hardens, and then she calls someone like me. Women like this sit in front of me with panic in their eyes because they are afraid that in the biggest decision of life they made a bad one. They married an arrogant, unyielding man, and they're hoping there is some way I can change their husband.

One woman in particular stands out in my mind. I wish I had it on tape. She said, "My husband doesn't listen to me. He is so arrogant. What can I do?"

I said, "Talk to him straight. You don't have anything to lose; tell him how deeply you're hurt when he doesn't listen to you."

She said, "What shouldn't I do?"

I said, "Are you punishing him sexually, cutting him off? Don't do that. Are you trying to manipulate him? Don't do that. You have to be what God wants you to be and let God change him."

Then she got a little gleam in her eye, looked at me, and said, "Can I kill him?"

"No!"

She was silent for a moment, then said, "Are you sure?"

I said, "Yeah, it's right here in the Bible. I've read it."

But that's the way she feels.

If your husband is hurting and says something to you, and you stomp off and close the door like a little girl, your marriage will be in trouble. You might stay together, you might go though the motions, but your mate will go outside of your marriage to find esteem and worth.

If you are treating your wife poorly, let me tell you the truth—she doesn't like you and she doesn't respect you. She feels you're a liar—you hooked her into this marriage under false pretenses and you defrauded her. I'll promise you she's looking someplace else for friendship and respect, and she may even be having fantasies about your premature death.

So when your mate is hurting, pay attention. When my wife says, "I'm hurt," I have learned to turn completely in her direction and give her my undivided attention. I hear her heart, and even though I often have no idea what to say, I step out and respond as best I know how.

Action 6: Trust One Another

Marriage needs trust. Don't make unwise overtures and create emotional intimacy with people of the opposite sex. Your spouse will worry and for a good reason. Don't have lunch alone with a member of the opposite sex. If your wife ever says to you that she feels like another woman is getting too close, don't argue. If your husband ever says he wants you to stop talking so much with another man, listen to him. You can't betray the trust of your mate.

But you also shouldn't doubt your mate for no reason. I have had people in my congregation who have been burdened by an unnecessary jealousy. Now if some guy gets too close to my wife, I would be jealous. That's not a bad thing. God is jealous for his bride.

But if I call home from San Antonio and my wife isn't there, and I call again at ten o'clock and she isn't there, I don't come home and say to this woman who has given me no reason to ever doubt her, "Where were you? Who did you see? Who were you with? Who was it?" That's just plain wicked. There is no reason in the world for me to doubt my wife.

Frankly, when I see a man who is continually suspicious and wounding the heart of his spouse, my thought is, *You have some serious issues.* Were you foolish enough to marry someone you can't trust? Or have you grown doubtful because of sin in your own heart? Unfounded jealousy will eat away at the core of a marriage. You have to trust your mate.

Action 7: Create Romance

I've never met a man who married a woman because he looked at her and said, "Now, that woman can keep a house." No woman said, "That's the mechanic I've prayed for all my life." No! You married your wife because she was pretty, sweet, and, hopefully, a godly woman. You looked into her eyes, and she melted your heart. At some point, you leaned over to her and said those words, "I love you." And it went so deeply into her heart that you wanted to get married right there. It felt so good to let somebody in so completely to your heart. That's why you got married.

But you did it then as an instinct. You have to do it now as a discipline. By that I mean you have to be affectionate with your mate. Husbands, touch your wife affectionately, not in a sexual way but just to show her you care. Wives, you don't have to wear the nightgown that was handed down from your mother and her mother before her. It's a great poncho, but you can buy something else. It means that you can sit on your husband's lap and look into his eyes and tell him "thank you."

My wife has a custom. I don't know where she got it, but I say "hallelujah." When a man's been out of the house for awhile and then comes home, she thinks he needs at least a ten-second kiss from his wife. That's a marvelous custom that we have. I guarantee that will put some steam in your stride when you come through the door.

We need affection from our spouses. Do you tell your mate that you love them? Tell her you love her, show her affection. Men, don't bring roses home only on Valentine's. Be spontaneous. If I give my wife roses on her birthday, I have met the basic level of her expectations. But if I come home from the store with a ninety-nine-cent plant one day, my wife glows.

Spontaneity—it means that you spend ridiculous amounts of money on your mate for no good reason, just to show how much you love them. It's the best investment you'll ever make.

Husbands also need to realize that acts of service are romantic. Men, if you get your motor running about nine o'clock at night and start thinking about being in bed with your wife, don't just take a shower and jump into bed like Sean Connery waiting for her to come into the room. What is she doing while you're laying there? She's cleaning up, locking the doors, and putting the kids to bed. Put the dishes in the dishwasher. Straighten up things around the house. Help your wife put the kids to bed. Do acts of service. As Laura Schlesinger says, "The sound of my husband vacuuming is foreplay."

Success in Marriage Comes from Applying Biblical Truth

In the fall of 1998, an anonymous donor in Florida had an idea. He wanted to hire an ad agency to design a campaign to get the people of his community talking about God. The Smith Agency designed eighteen billboards with sayings from God and purchased more than $100,000 worth of billboard space around the city. With sayings like "Let's meet at My house Sunday before the game," the signs were an immediate phenomenon.

What happened next is the hand of God. In the spring of 1999, the Outdoor Advertising Agency of America for some reason decided to use the spiritual billboards for its public service campaign that year. Soon, the sayings from God were appearing on ten thousand billboards around the country free of charge.

My favorite billboard is the one that says, "The wedding was nice. How about inviting me to the marriage? God." Americans still get flowery and spiritual in our weddings; we're just not real good at bringing God into our marriages. He wants to be invited to your marriage.

Let me give you an illustration. A few years ago we had twenty men from our congregation go to Honduras to build a church. These men were not just old pack mules that could move cement blocks; we sent master craftsmen. One man had a degree in architecture from the University of Texas. Another man was a master mason. Another is a top contractor in the area. Another man is a master carpenter.

We sent these talented men down to help the people in Honduras build a church. Little did we realize that in Honduras most things are not built by master craftsmen. This church was no exception. They were just taking cement and cinder blocks and some support lumber and putting it up. They were building it quickly, like a hut.

They didn't know our people from Adam. They had no idea these Americans were top craftsmen who had the knowledge and skills to do the job right. The man they had in charge was directing everything in Spanish, and our men graciously jumped right in and helped any way they could. They had a great time, won some people to Christ, and had a blessed time of ministry.

Still, the fact is the amateurs were doing the planning and leading, while the skilled craftsmen were just helping out. The foundation was poured incorrectly, so it wasn't square. The walls were out of plumb, but they were trying their best. They put up beams that were not really strong enough to support the trusses, so our guys added strength where they could. They told me afterward, "Even though we knew so much and had so much to give, the most we could do was damage control." It almost drove them crazy.

Too often, this is the way our marriages are with God. He can build it correctly the first time from the ground up, but we just use Him for damage control. Why don't you say to God what the

Hondurans should have said to our craftsmen? "Tell you what, I haven't done so well. Why don't You build it and tell me what to do." If you're messing up in your marriage, everything else you're doing in the Christian life is for show because you're dead right where you stand. Don't go to church next week if you haven't dealt with this because it will just be for show.

If you need to, let today be the day you get back with God in your marriage. Put this book down and look into the eyes of your mate and repent. Let God bring some tears and get yourselves right under the authority of God. And then call some friends in to help you along. You cannot be happy in life when your marriage is in trouble.

Biblical success comes when you

1. let your fear of God determine your attitude toward your spouse,
2. understand and celebrate the roles of a man and woman in marriage,
3. follow through on your responsibilities,
4. stay committed to your marriage no matter what,
5. treat your spouse with courtesy and esteem, experience Level 3 communication, spend time together, deal with conflict, trust one another, and create romance.

A PRAYER FOR TRUE SUCCESS

Father, we want to do marriage right. We know that this is very close to Your heart. We know that marriage is a precious gift, so help us treat it with honor and respect every day. Help us to love our spouses with a sacrificial love that honors You. Though we fail, You give grace. Allow us to take that grace and turn it to joy in our marriages for Your glory. We ask this in Jesus' name. Amen.

THINKING MORE DEEPLY ABOUT TRUE SUCCESS

1. What are some of the different views people have about marriage today? What impact have some of these views had on our culture?

2. Why is the fear of God foundational to marriage? When your relationship with God is not right, how does that affect your other relationships? How do you turn that around?

3. What happens in a marriage when spouses forget their roles or responsibilities? Has this ever happened to you? What did you learn?

4. Which of the seven actions mentioned in this chapter are you doing the best at in your marriage? With which action do you need the most improvement? What steps can you take?

CHAPTER 11

Children:

Eight Essential Vitamins for Your Kids

For years, food products have been boasting that they are "fortified with eight essential vitamins and minerals." In the case of many cereals, that's a good thing because they sure don't have many nutrients on their own.

In this chapter, I want to help you learn eight essential spiritual vitamins that your children need to receive. If your children get these, they will grow up spiritually strong and healthy. If they don't, they will wither and die.

The stakes in parenting are huge. This is your legacy—you'll be dealing with your children and their children for the rest of your life. How you are doing as a parent also colors every aspect of your life. No matter what I'm going through, I feel pretty good as long as my wife and children are doing OK. You could lose your job or even your health, and it will be all right as long as your family is following God. "A wise son makes a father glad" (Prov. 10:1).

That's why we need to add parenting to our list of critical characteristics that make up a biblically successful life:

a foundation of fearing God and gathering wisdom
the ability to maintain relationships
values
integrity
self-control
submission to authority
shock absorbers to deal with difficult times
positive peer pressure
a correct view of work
a biblically healthy marriage
biblical parenting skills

Before we get started, I realize that people can feel a tremendous amount of guilt about their kids. None of us are where we ought to be as parents. I know I could have done a better job. Now that mine are grown, I should probably adopt four or five because I know so much more about what I ought to have done. (It may just be that the farther away I get from it, the less I remember how hard it is.)

In this chapter I want to help you understand how you can find success with your children. But I don't want you to be covered up with guilt. Don't underline three sentences on every page of this chapter and leave it where your spouse can find it. Basically, the way to find success as a parent is to take the lessons of the rest of this book and instill them in your children. Sometimes that is easier said than done, isn't it?

Here are eight essential vitamins that will help your children absorb the lessons of true biblical success.

Vitamin 1: Peace

Was your home peaceful when you were a child? Praise God if it was. "Better is a dry morsel and quietness with it than a house full of feasting with strife" (Prov. 17:1).

Many people grew up in homes marked by consistent explosions of anger between their parents. They saw sporadic fighting and frequent unresolved conflicts. A lot of parents chose not to deal with this conflict and just acted as if nothing happened. In that environment, the children are forced to walk on eggshells because they don't want to be the ones to set off the next explosion.

A lot of kids can't wait to graduate high school to get away from the arguments at home. When they turn eighteen, they head for the city-limits sign as fast as they can to try to find some peace.

The most valuable thing I provide for my children is to consistently demonstrate love for my wife. A child can forgive almost any sin so long as his parents love each other. Peace and affection between parents provide a stable foundation for your children. They need their home to be a safe haven from the storms around them. Your first responsibility is to create an environment of peace.

Never heatedly argue with your spouse in front of your children. Watch your tone of voice. Don't be condescending or harsh. Discuss the issues while treating your partner with respect. It's good for kids to see parents work through conflict, but if you feel the need to raise your voice or get overly emotional, then go back into the bedroom to talk it out. Don't rob your children of the peace of their home. They are not emotionally ready to handle adult emotions.

Don't play the part of a spoiled brat, freezing out your spouse instead of working through conflict. Children pick up on these patterns. They feel the tension just underneath the surface. They also don't learn healthy patterns of dealing with conflict in their own lives.

I've had to apologize to my children at times. I've had to go into my son's room and say, "I've sinned against your mom. I didn't treat her with the respect God tells me to, and I want to ask you to forgive me." My sweet wife has gone to my sons and done the same thing.

If you don't submit to God's authority over your marriage, what makes you think your children will submit to your authority? They know you are supposed to treat your spouse with respect. They know you aren't supposed to degrade and belittle or henpeck each other. So when they see that happening, they lose all respect and any desire to submit to your authority. Your children need to see consistency between the propositional truth you teach them and the truth they see incarnate in your life. They need to grow up in a safe environment where Mom and Dad love one another.

One of the things I am most grateful for is that my mother made my childhood home a magical place. There was such love and happiness in my home. I especially remember the traditions we followed. She made Christmas wonderful, Easter amazing, Thanksgiving a joy—even losing a tooth was a treat. I believed in the tooth fairy until I was twenty-two!

My home was so special that when I left for college, the last thing I took with me was a rock that I put in my pocket. Every time I felt homesick or lonely at college, I reached in my pocket and felt that rock. It was a little piece of home. Even today in times of turmoil, my heart goes back to Waco, Texas.

Giving your child a peaceful home builds a foundation for long-term success.

After reading this section, you may need to put this book down and spend some time with God. And then you may need to get with your spouse and go to your children and ask their forgiveness. Do whatever it takes to make your home a place of peace.

Vitamin 2: Time

In 2 Samuel 14, we read the story of what happens after David's son Absalom murdered his half-brother Amnon. Absalom ran away after the confrontation, and David was persuaded by Joab to receive Absalom back. But when Absalom returned, notice what David did. "Now Absalom lived two full years in Jerusalem, and did not see the king's face" (2 Sam. 14:28). In other words, David said, "I'll bring you back to the city since I have to, but I am not going to spend time with you or talk to you."

How did Absalom respond? "Then Absalom sent for Joab, to send him to the king, but he would not come to him. So he sent again a second time, but he would not come" (2 Sam. 14:29). This young man is trying to get his father to spend time with him, to talk with him, and to forgive him. He wants to know that his father loves him. He knows that his father is a marvelous divine administrator. I'm sure he was thinking, *My dad has time to talk to everybody in Israel but his son*. Sound familiar?

What does Absalom do? He sets Joab's field on fire—that's a good way to get your daddy to notice you. "I'll burn his administrator's field, then we'll see if he will listen to me." We see this same thing today, with children crying out for attention through acts of rebellion. Piercings, tattoos, drugs, shoplifting, failing grades—often these are signs that a child wants someone to pay attention to them.

It worked partially for Absalom. Joab came and asked him why he set his field on fire. "Absalom answered Joab, 'Behold, I sent for you, saying, "Come here, that I may send you to the king, to say, 'Why have I come from Geshur? It would be better for me still to be there.'" Now therefore, let me see the king's face, and if there is iniquity in me, let him put me to death.' So when Joab came to the king and told him, he called for Absalom. Thus he came to the king and prostrated himself on his face to the ground before the king, and the king kissed Absalom" (2 Sam. 14:32–33).

Absalom was saying he might as well have lived on the other side of the nation as to live in a city where his father would not talk to him.

The second vitamin a child needs is time. He needs a father and mother to look at him full in the face and listen to him. There are times when a child needs to be lectured, and there are times when a child needs simply to be listened to and loved and valued.

Unfortunately one of the most terrifying things for many children is to spend time with their fathers. Either their father ignores them and acts like they are not there, or their father takes them on a three-hour car ride, locks the doors, and preaches to them. Nothing could be worse for your relationship with your child. A child needs time where he or she is getting our full attention.

Nothing will make a grown man or woman break down faster than talking about the time that their mom or dad spent with them. I've seen grown men break down weeping and have to be led from the stage. I know I can't do it. I can remember distinctly the times Daddy and I went dove hunting even when I didn't shoot a dove.

I remember one time I shot my daddy in the rear end. We were hunting on the Bosque River. He was on the sandbar, and I was on the shore. The dove flew down between us, and I put my shotgun right on that dove and "boom." Fortunately, Daddy was far enough away that he only got hit with some that skipped off the water.

I can remember fishing with my father. I can remember cold coffee grounds on an open fire. I can remember listening to my father tell stories of baseball games. These are the times that helped shape who I am today.

Spend time with your children. Don't lecture your child unless there is the need. Love him and laugh at his jokes.

Jonathan Edwards, the great pastor and theologian of the Great Awakening, had thirteen children. It is said that every day he would set aside time to spend with his wife and with one child. This allowed him to spend time with each of his kids every couple of weeks. Time is precious to your children.

What is the best way to raise a child? It's the same way you raise a golden retriever. If you want to have a good dog, after it's born, you put it in your pocket and take that little doggie with you every place you go. You put it in your pickup, you put it in a cab, put it in your car, put it in your home, and when it grows up, that dog will never leave your side.

If you will take your little child with you wherever you go, you will build a precious future. Fathers, there is no amount of success in this world that is ever going to replace the pain of a child gone bad. And there is no amount of pain in this world that can take away the joy of a godly boy or a godly girl.

Vitamin 3: Truth

Scriptures are clear that we need to immerse our children in the truth (see Deut. 6; Prov. 3; and Eph. 6). Scripture also gives us an example of what this looks like when it happens.

Paul is writing to Timothy, warning him about the difficulties Timothy will face in his ministry. In chapter 3 of his second letter, he tells Timothy there will be challenges to the Word of God. Paul tells him difficult times will come (3:1) and that he should continue in his belief in the Word of God (3:14). Why does Paul say Timothy should do these things? Because Timothy has known about them since childhood: "From childhood you have known the sacred writings which are able to give you the wisdom that leads to salvation through faith which is in Christ Jesus" (2 Tim. 3:15). How did Timothy learn Scripture as a child? From his grandmother Lois and his mother Eunice (2 Tim. 1:5). One of the most steadfast leaders of the early church became a pillar because his grandmother and mother taught him the truth.

I wish I had done even more of this with my children. Even though I knew Scripture taught this, I still underestimated the impact of what I was doing while I was doing it. It's so easy when you are teaching a bedtime story to your child to think you are not doing anything important. It doesn't seem that critical when you are praying with your little bitty girl or little bitty boy. But these things are absolutely vital. This is the foundation on which everything else is built.

Read children's books of Bible stories to your kids. They need to know about Shadrach, Meshach, Abednego, and Daniel. They need to have stories of moral guidance. Pray intelligently with your children at meals and at night time. Pray with them theologically—they won't even know they are getting good teaching. Don't just say, "Thank You for the burrito. Amen." You can do better.

Let me tell you how my mother did this for me. When I was eleven years old, I didn't make the all-star team. It was a crushing blow. I had three buddies who did, and it killed me. My mother sat down with me on a bed, patted my back, and told me the story of Joseph. She told me how God gave him a promise, and when everything went south on him, he kept hanging in there. One day God fulfilled His promise and raised Joseph to the highest position in the land. I have never forgotten that day or that story.

You can't teach your child the truth if you don't have peace in your home. You can't teach your child the truth if you don't spend time with them. But you also can't teach your child the truth if you don't live out the truth yourself.

Vitamin 4: An Example

When Paul wrote to Timothy, he was able to point to the example of Timothy's grandmother Lois and mother Eunice. Timothy's life and faith was shaped by the way his mother and grandmother lived.

The fourth essential vitamin for your children is an example. Never underestimate what it means for your child to see you hug your spouse or for your child to hear you pray. Has your child ever walked in on you when you were on your knees before God? Are you the most godly man or woman that your child has ever met? If not, why not?

A living example imprints truth into a child. They are molded and shaped by it; they absorb it through their pores. The things they learn from your example will never leave. To this day I can vividly remember the way my mother and father lived out their love for us. They were at our ball games. They helped with our schoolwork. They lived their lives so that what they did matched what they said.

Vitamin 5: Esteem

A consistent example will help your child build a proper view of himself. One of the great tasks of a growing up is figuring out who you are. How can you help your kids grow up with a biblical esteem for their worth as children of God?

Paul says, "Fathers, do not exasperate your children, so that they will not lose heart" (Col. 3:21). It's easy for parents to unintentionally create an environment that exasperates and discourages children. Children who believe there is no way they can please their parents lose their passion and ambition. If they can't live up to your expectations, eventually they will quit trying. Esteem means you love your child no matter what.

A child needs to know that he is loved and accepted for exactly who he is. This is how he gains a proper understanding of who God has made him to be. This holds true even when we realize our children are different from us—or maybe even different from what we always dreamed they would be. Whether your son is an athlete or a scientist, he should feel the same unconditional love. Whether your daughter is a tomboy or a cheerleader, she should know that there is no way you will ever stop loving her.

I've already mentioned that I was an athlete growing up, and my son Benjamin loved to play sports when he was little. When he got older, he decided to go into the military, something I know nothing about. But when he graduated at Fort Benning, I emptied the bank account to fly our whole family out there just to watch him get the blue cord of the infantry put on his shoulder. When he saw his father, mother, and grandparents in the crowd, he knew we were just as proud of him excelling at Fort Benning as we were with him on any other kind of field.

Send your children this message: "You can be the person God has made you to be and I will always love you." When your child is struggling, take her in your arms and tell her, "I'm proud of you." Write down fifty different ways to say it and use them all: "I'm so glad God allowed me to be your mom," "I thank God every day for giving you to us," "You are such a precious part of our family."

Don't let your child lose heart.

Help your children see themselves as God sees them by celebrating who they are. "Train up a child in the way he should go, even when he is old he will not depart from it" (Prov. 22:6). A major aspect of this verse is often misinterpreted. Some take it to mean that you need to teach your children the right thing, and when they are older, they will do it. This verse means much more than that. We need to raise up a child in his particular bent, being sensitive to his particular uniqueness. The verse literally says, "Raise up a child in his way."

Did your mother ever say to you, "How come you can't work hard like your brother?" Or "Why don't you do well in school like your sister?" Even if you didn't say it, you thought it—*Because I'm not my sister*. Don't try to make your flat-footed boy be a high jumper because his older brother was. Ask the same question that Samson's parents did: "Lord, what shall his vocation be?" Have you asked the Lord that for your children?

Your child is created in God's image, not yours. He is on loan to you from God. You figure out why God made him and then develop those characteristics every way you can. Support who your child decides to be. A child needs to know that you love her and that you're excited about how God made her. She doesn't need to feel that you're frustrated that God didn't do better. Train your children up in the way God gave them to you.

Vitamin 6: Acceptance

If esteem is loving your child no matter who he is, then acceptance is loving your child no matter what he does. A child must know that a parent always loves even if the parent is not always pleased. This is the way God loves us.

When a child senses that his parent's love ebbs and flows based on what he does, he eventually becomes a neurotic child. A son will always be left wondering whether he has done enough this time to earn the attention and affection that he craves. A young daughter who can't find acceptance and unconditional love at home will look for places where she feels loved no matter what she does.

If, as Solomon says, "A friend loves at all times" (Prov. 17:17), how much more a parent? Remember the prodigal son in Jesus' parable. As soon as the son made the move to come home, his father ran to meet him and swept him up in forgiveness and love. Another way to see that story is that it is about a "prodigal" father because the word *prodigal* (from "prodigious") can mean "excessive." The father was excessive in his love and forgiveness and acceptance of his son.

Tolerating your children is not the same as accepting them. We need to be excessive in our forgiveness and love in a way that makes our children understand our deep and abiding unconditional love. Do your children feel tolerated or celebrated? Just like Absalom set fire to the field to get his father's acceptance, so children still light fires to make parents respond to their hurts and fears today.

Vitamin 7: Affection

Affection is love with skin on it. Your children need a mom and dad who hold them. I tell young fathers to keep hugging their little daughter even as she gets older. It might feel kind of awkward when this sixteen-year-old comes and sits beside you for a hug, but she needs to always know the wonderful, normal feeling of her father's affection.

Fathers, it's tough when you love your boys. You hug on them when they are little and soft and cuddly, but then they get kind of old and pimply and greasy. Even when you don't feel like hugging them, wrestle with them. Grab them and roll around, but always keep close to your boys. Walk up to them and put your hand on their shoulder and squeeze. Let them know Dad still thinks they are special even though they are becoming men.

When I came to Christ, there were a number of great big, greasy football players who came to the Lord around the same time. We all went to the same church, and this little old lady there would hug us. We would all go over to her house, and she would fix us cucumbers, pork chops, salad, and sweetened ice tea. We would go because she was willing to cook for us but also because she hugged us and said she loved us. I remember looking around the church and seeing this little old lady sitting on a pew surrounded by these big men. She owned them because she loved them. Keep your hands on your kids.

Vitamin 8: Discipline

Every child is born as a flawed instrument. This is why the Bible stressed the role of proper discipline for our children. "He who withholds his rod hates his son, but he who loves him disciplines him diligently" (Prov. 13:24). Something is wrong with our children because something is wrong with their parents. When the sperm and egg come together, they make a flawed being. They inherit a sinful nature. We can all say like David, "Behold, I was brought forth in iniquity, and in sin my mother conceived me" (Ps. 51:5).

Even secular culture is recognizing the need for discipline in the lives of our children. *Newsweek* magazine recently had a cover story on the effects of permissive parenting. They cited a survey that showed that children expect to ask their parents nine times for something new before their parents give in. And parents are spending more and more for nonessential items for their children—$53.8 billion in 2004, $17.6 billion more than in 1997.[1]

Our children need to hear the word *no*. Solomon said, "He who withholds his rod hates his son, but he who loves him disciplines him diligently" (Prov. 13:24). The opposite of love is not hate. The opposite of love is apathy. Many children are growing up in homes where their parents simply do not care enough to discipline them.

Start disciplining your children when they are young. "Discipline your son while there is hope, and do not desire his death" (Prov. 19:18). Create the patterns and habits of righteous behavior in your children from an early age. If you don't, what starts as a little problem with a three-year-old will be an unmitigated disaster with a seventeen-year-old.

For example, don't ever let your children get in the habit of disrespecting their mother. Jump on them with both feet right then and take them aside, saying, "Young man/lady, there are a lot of things you can do. But don't you ever disrespect the woman God gave me as a wife."

Gang up on your children and work together for good. Be unified in your approach to discipline. Some of the best child-rearing advice I've ever heard has come from Dr. James Dobson. He gave the example of a football referee. What does he do when a player jumps offsides? He doesn't get red-faced, screaming about the virtues of keeping the rules. He drops the flag and steps off the penalty. When your child messes up, don't break the peace of your home; just step off the penalty. Do it consistently. Don't reason with a little child; they will find a way to string the discussion out.

And contrary to what popular culture says, there is a time when a good spanking is appropriate. Children get "earwax buildup," so that they don't listen to their parents. One solution is to heat their bottom about ten degrees and see how fast it melts that wax.

"Do not hold back discipline from the child, although you strike him with the rod, he will not die" (Prov. 23:13). Don't fear your child's tears. They can either cry a few tears now from discipline or cry buckets of tears later when they make a disaster of their lives. Those tears now will dry up. The ones twenty years from now—when they have mangled their lives with bad marriages, jobs, and choices—will soak their pillowcases and sheets. They can cry a little now or weep bitterly later.

"The rod and reproof give wisdom, but a child who gets his own way brings shame to his mother" (Prov. 29:15). If you can't discipline your children for their own good, at least do it for your own good, so they don't embarrass you. Without discipline your child will grow up to be a selfish, miserable adult.

But discipline is more than just prohibiting certain behaviors. Often Christian parents think they are doing a good job because they don't let their kids behave in certain ways or watch certain movies or go to certain places. Setting boundaries is certainly a part of parenting, but you also need to have a positive agenda for your children. Short of raising them in a cave on a cliff in a desert somewhere, there is no way you are going to keep your children untouched by the world. It is not going to happen. They will eventually have to deal with a world that hates Christ and promotes the unashamed love of self. It's not enough to be on the defensive—your children need to be on the offensive to fight for Christ's kingdom in this world. That's why your children need these eight essential vitamins not only to inoculate them from the world but also to help them become mighty warriors for Christ.

Biblical success comes when you

1. create a peaceful home,
2. spend time with your children,
3. instill the truths of God's Word in your children,
4. provide an example to your children,
5. help your children see themselves as God sees them,
6. accept your children no matter what they do,
7. show affection to your children,
8. discipline your children so they will gain wisdom.

A PRAYER FOR TRUE SUCCESS

Father, You have bestowed on us the greatest responsibility of our lives—the shaping of the lives of our children. Help us craft and direct these arrows in our quiver so they fly straight and true. Give us the grace to teach them truly, to model truth faithfully, and to correct our children whenever a breach is made. May we care more about their eternal souls than their temporary happiness. We ask this in Jesus' name. Amen.

THINKING MORE DEEPLY ABOUT TRUE SUCCESS

1. Looking at our culture today, what do you think are some of the most common mistakes made in parenting? What are their consequences?

2. Did you grow up in a peaceful home? How did it affect you? Why is a good home so important for children?

3. If you had to choose one word to describe the contribution your parents made to your life, what would it be? Why?

4. What is the difference between esteem and acceptance? Why are these both so important to children? How can you help give them to your children or grandchildren?

5. What are your goals for your children or grandchildren? Have you settled for hoping they won't turn out too bad, or are you praying for warriors who can change the world for Christ? How could this change of perspective impact your interactions with your children or grandchildren?

CHAPTER 12

Money:

Handle or Be Handled by Wealth

For the last forty years, scientists have been researching ways to restore hearing to people who are deaf. After decades of dead ends, they finally found success with the cochlear implant.

This device is amazing. A surgeon implants a receiver in the skull behind the ear and then drills a hole through the bone to the cochlea. Electrodes are then placed in the cochlea to stimulate the auditory nerves.

A microphone worn behind the ear picks up sound, and a computer converts the sound into electronic signals and transmits them wirelessly to the receiver inside the skull. Many people with severe hearing loss can now recover more than 80 percent of their hearing with the use of these implants. What a marvel!

I have a friend who is one of the leading surgeons in the United States in performing this operation. He makes a lot of money. Our society greatly values people who can drill holes in your head, install a computer, and give you back your hearing. But how long do you think it takes him to perform his part of the actual surgery? One hour!

I think I'll start doing that after I finish this book—sounds like a good deal. Just cut them open, pop the little doodad in there, and sew them back up.

Of course, it is not that easy—my friend studied for a dozen years to be able to do what he does. And he deserves every penny he earns.

I am not an ENT surgical specialist; I'm a pastor. In our culture, there is a basic range of income that a pastor makes. The same thing is true for mechanics, school teachers, bank managers, and copier salesmen. I can choose to be bitter that, as a pastor, I don't make as much money as my friend, or I can choose to appreciate what God has given me.

You are faced with the same temptation every day. One thing I can assure you—you'll never be all you can be unless you conquer this temptation and learn to handle your money.

So we need to add a proper view of money to our list of what it takes to find biblical success.

a foundation of fearing God and gathering wisdom
the ability to maintain relationships
values
integrity
self-control
submission to authority
shock absorbers to deal with difficult times
positive peer pressure
a correct view of work
a biblically healthy marriage
biblical parenting skills
a proper view of money

God deals us different hands. Some people are tall and others short. Some are smart and others a little slow. Some have the ability to make a lot of money and others just plod along.

The Bible says, "It is [God] who is giving you power to make wealth" (Deut. 8:18). It's OK that we are all different. That's the hand I've been dealt, and that's the hand you've been dealt. Play your hand. If I have food and covering I shall be content. Are you suffering because you don't have a second jet ski, or a first one for that matter? Are you suffering because you don't have a getaway in Vail? It would be nice to have one, but somehow I think we will survive without one.

Materialism has nothing to do with how much you own or how much you make; it has everything to do with how you regard money and how you use it. You can be a fool making minimum wage, or you can be godly making a million dollars a year. It's all how you use and regard your money.

Paul tells us the proper attitude to have toward money. "Instruct those who are rich in this present world not to be conceited or to fix their hope on the uncertainty of riches, but on God, who richly supplies us with all things to enjoy. Instruct them to do good, to be rich in good works, to be generous and ready to share, storing up for themselves the treasure of a good foundation for the future, so that they may take hold of that which is life indeed" (1 Tim. 6:17–19). Paul tells us we will have biblical success with money if we do three things: enjoy it, use it, and invest it. But he also shows us two bad things that can happen to us and our money.

Don't Be Conceited

"Instruct those who are rich in this present world not to be conceited." When you make money, it's easy to believe that you made it happen in your own strength. We actually idolize this in America—the rags-to-riches stories, the self-made man. The problem is that this kind of attitude quickly turns to arrogance and conceit.

When you are conceited, you begin to treat others as underlings. "The rich man answers roughly," says Proverbs 18:23. You are so focused on yourself and your agenda that you naturally think first about how another person can help you. People around you become tools you can use to reach the goals you have set. All of a sudden, you have taken God's gifts to you and used them to elevate yourself above those around you.

This conceit can even be institutionalized as a virtue. There is a social club for elite singles in central Florida that advertises a minimum salary for male members of $100,000 a year. The founder of the club says she is trying to preserve the upper echelon. "The lower socioeconomic class is doing fine. They can meet in laundromats," she says. But the highest class of people are "not meeting, mating, and procreating."[1]

This is the kind of world we live in—the vices of snobbery and materialism are turned into virtues. That's what money will do to you if you are not careful.

Paul says, "What do you have that you did not receive? And if you did receive it, why do you boast as if you had not received it?" (1 Cor. 4:7). Be very careful if you have more money than someone else. Don't let it go to your head. Don't be conceited.

Don't Depend on Money for Your Future

Paul also says not to fix your hope on the uncertainty of riches. In the Bible, the word *hope* has a different meaning than we typically give it in English—which is more "wish" than "hope," as in, "I hope it doesn't rain." Biblically, hope is the assurance of a future event that is certain to happen. You can count on it.

For example, we are to be "looking for the blessed hope and the appearing of the glory of our great God and Savior, Christ Jesus" (Titus 2:13). Peter says to "fix your hope completely on the grace to be brought to you at the revelation of Jesus Christ" (1 Pet. 1:13). Widows should fix their hope on God (1 Tim. 5). Paul could labor and strive in the ministry because he had fixed his hope on the living God (1 Tim. 4:10).

We can be certain of only one thing, and it is not money. The only thing you can be certain of is God. He is the only one who is unchanging and eternal. If you put your hope in anything else—especially money—you are a fool.

Can you be certain you will be alive tomorrow? Can you be certain that you won't lose your job? That you won't lose all your money in a bad investment or a lawsuit?

This text tells us that money has a dangerous propensity. Money seduces us into believing that it can support the weight of our dreams and hopes. But it can't. It's like quicksand that pulls us down after we step on it with both feet.

What was the most significant event of 1929? In September and October of that year, the U.S. stock market lost more than 40 percent of its value, causing a ripple effect through the world economy. By the summer of 1932, the market had stabilized but was down almost 90 percent from its previous high. What happened to people who put their hope in the uncertainty of riches? Some of them jumped out of windows of high-rise buildings to their deaths.

Of course, that was way back then and it could never happen again, right? Actually the worst day in stock market history in terms of percentage decline was Black Monday, October 19, 1987, when the market fell 22.6 percent in one day. Don't put your hope in money. It can't deliver on its promises.

You Won't Find Biblical Success through Debt

A lot of people are in trouble financially because they place their hope in money in more subtle ways. People make money and immediately go out and spend it on things they want but don't really need. When they reach the end of their earnings, they use credit cards to spend more and begin piling up consumer debt. In 2001, the Federal Reserve estimated that Americans averaged more than $13,000 in credit-card debt per household.

Now a lot of those people wish they had never heard of credit cards. The things they bought have long since worn out, but they are still paying for them every month.

Debt distracts us from important things. When you are in debt, you have what you haven't earned, and now you're obligated to pay that person back in the future. The Bible says that "the borrower becomes the lender's slave" (Prov. 22:7). When you take debt, you give up freedom. There are certain things you can't do anymore because you are obligated in future days to pay back that money.

Debt is like a pet anaconda. It seems pretty harmless at first, but when you begin to feed it, the snake gets bigger and wraps itself around you, eventually crushing you. All of your dreams for the future and all of your joy can be crushed under the mountain of your financial obligations. It's no fun when you have to pay the fiddler, and every month he gets louder and louder. I like fiddle music as much as the next guy, but not when you hear it all night long in your bedroom. Nothing will keep you up at night like living in debt.

Live within Your Income

Play the hand that you are dealt. Don't go out and get things you can't afford.

This is a huge issue for younger adults. Many folks assume that upon graduation from college, they are going to start out with the lifestyle their parents have. The truth is your dad worked for thirty years to accumulate that nice house and new car every three years. If you are making $30,000 a year out of college, you don't get to have the toys your daddy has. You have to work your way up the system.

I see lots of young couples become bitter because they are not able to live at the standard to which they have been accustomed. Often, they start living beyond their income and sink themselves in debt. "An inheritance gained hurriedly at the beginning will not be blessed in the end" (Prov. 20:21). In other words, kids who get too much too quick get messed up.

If you're a wife, don't pressure your husband to make more money. He'll try to do it by working eighty hours a week, which will negatively affect your family cohesion. Don't pressure him in subtle ways—making plans for expensive furniture or trips that are beyond what you can afford. He'll want to please you and find a way to earn that extra money. And if he doesn't, he'll be tempted to go into debt to give them to you anyway.

If you're a husband, don't make your wife work so you can have more toys. If your wife chooses to work, and you can balance it as a couple, then that is your privilege. But it is not your wife's obligation. It is your obligation. Working is very difficult for most women if they feel like they are losing out on being a good wife and mother simply to have more optional stuff.

The Danger of Double Incomes

When your wife works, you have an extra income and more money. (Of course, nobody actually wants to make more money; they want to spend more money.) So you can easily get used to living at the level of those two incomes . . . even though one of them may go away.

When they have children, many women want to stay home and be with them. "I don't want to let someone else raise my child. What's the use of having a child if I can't shape them?" And so she wants to quit work. However, when the parents look at their budget, they realize there is no way they will make it on one income. So now they have to decide—the child or the Chrysler? Currently in our culture, the Chrysler is winning. And there are a lot of bitter, regret-filled women who hate the compromises they feel like they were forced to make.

Through Paul, God warns us not to become arrogant and also not to put our hope in money. In addition to giving us these two warnings, Paul also shows us three things God wants us to do with our money.

Enjoy It

Paul says in 1 Timothy 6:17 that God "richly supplies us with all things to enjoy." One of the primary reasons God gives us money is to enjoy it.

Asceticism is the belief that you should deny yourself pleasure in order to be more holy. You don't eat any food that tastes good. You don't get married and make love to your spouse. You don't sleep in a bed with a soft pillow; you find a cold, hard cave and a rock with a few sharp points on it. Deny the body any comfort or pleasure and you will be made pure.

This philosophy is an unbiblical heresy that will keep you from lasting success.

There are actually more biblical mandates to enjoy your money than there are to save it. Is it biblical to have insurance? Yes. Should you save for your kids? Of course. Should you put money into retirement accounts to provide for you and your spouse later in life? Yes. But don't build your life on these things.

Too many people are simply enduring life rather than enjoying it. Don't just save money for the new vacuum cleaner, start setting aside some bungee-jumping money or some white-water rafting money. Instead of spending all your money on perishable things that will rot, spend your money on a ski trip with the family.

The things you buy are not the things that will bring your family closer together. Your family will be brought together by common laughter and common tears. You want common tears, go camping. I know that from experience.

Taking my family skiing has been one of the best things I have ever done. All of my goods will rot, but my memories can't be touched. That's why I tell young couples, "Don't go out and get a fancy leased car and a big house and expensive furniture. Take your money and go skiing, see the Grand Canyon, head to the islands, and take a million pictures while you're there." Use your money to build eternal memories.

As previously mentioned, I make a habit of asking older folks, "If you had it to do all over again, what would you do differently?" Almost every time I get a variation of the same answer. "I would not worry as much and I would take more risks"—which means, "I would enjoy right now." The future is a very uncertain thing. It's a low-rent commodity. You shouldn't live for it, and you can't trust it. Live today. Tomorrow's worries will take care of themselves. The ironic thing is that you live for eternity not by focusing on the future but rather by enjoying today.

If you aren't going to enjoy your money, you may as well stop making it. An old sage in our church says, "Make sure you run out of air and money at the same time." Another old buddy of mine said, "Make sure your last check bounces."

Use Your Money for Good

Paul tells us to enjoy our money, but he also tells us to use our money wisely. "Instruct them to do good, to be rich in good works, to be generous and ready to share" (1 Tim. 6:18). Hold your money loosely. Use your money to accomplish good in the world.

How should you use your money? The first principle is clear from the Bible: when you get your check, give at least 10 percent right off the top to the Lord. "Honor the Lord from your wealth and from the first of all your produce; so your barns will be filled with plenty and your vats will overflow with new wine" (Prov. 3:9–10).

God will always take care of you if you are willing to give. "Give, and it will be given to you. They will pour into your lap a good measure—pressed down, shaken together, and running over. For by your standard of measure it will be measured to you in return" (Luke 6:38). "Now this I say, he who sows sparingly will also reap sparingly, and he who sows bountifully will also reap bountifully" (2 Cor. 9:6). This doesn't mean you should use giving to God as an investment program. He doesn't promise to make you rich, just to take care of you.

You can also use your money for other good works. Do you have a system for spontaneous giving? Let me challenge you: the next time you meet someone with a financial need, just give them twenty bucks. See how it feels. Hold the money you have in your pocket with very loose fingers. Paul says to "be generous and ready to share" (1 Tim. 6:18).

Using Your Money to Invest for the Kingdom

Why should you use your money for good? Why give it away to the church and to people in need? Is it to make a noble sacrifice? Is it to make yourselves miserable and poor, so somehow you can be more holy or loved by God? Absolutely not. It's to store up eternal treasure.

Jesus tells a great parable that illustrates this point.

Now He was also saying to the disciples, "There was a rich man who had a manager, and this manager was reported to him as squandering his possessions.

"And he called him and said to him, 'What is this I hear about you? Give an accounting of your management, for you can no longer be manager.'

"The manager said to himself, 'What shall I do, since my master is taking the management away from me? I am not strong enough to dig; I am ashamed to beg.

'I know what I shall do, so that when I am removed from the management people will welcome me into their homes.'

"And he summoned each one of his master's debtors, and he began saying to the first, 'How much do you owe my master?'

"And he said, 'A hundred measures of oil.' And he said to him, 'Take your bill, and sit down quickly and write fifty.'

"Then he said to another, 'And how much do you owe?' And he said, 'A hundred measures of wheat.' He said to him, 'Take your bill, and write eighty.'

"And his master praised the unrighteous manager because he had acted shrewdly; for the sons of this age are more shrewd in relation to their own kind than the sons of light.

"And I say to you, make friends for yourselves by means of the wealth of unrighteousness, so that when it fails, they will receive you into the eternal dwellings.

"He who is faithful in a very little thing is faithful also in much; and he who is unrighteous in a very little thing is unrighteous also in much. Therefore if you have not been faithful in the use of unrighteous wealth, who will entrust the true riches to you? And if you have not been faithful in the use of that which is another's, who will give you that which is your own?

"No servant can serve two masters; for either he will hate the one and love the other, or else he will be devoted to one and despise the other. You cannot serve God and wealth."

Now the Pharisees, who were lovers of money, were listening to all these things and were scoffing at Him. (Luke 16:1–14)

What is Jesus' point? Did the master praise the manager because he was lazy and crooked? No, he praised him because he was ingenious, or "shrewd." I'm sure he wished the guy would have put as much thought into managing his resources as he did into what he would do after he was fired.

Jesus was saying that people who believe money only counts in the here and now are often more shrewd about how they use it than Christians, i.e., "the sons of light." They are smarter in using it for the things they believe than Christians are in using it for the things they believe.

Ask yourself this question on a daily basis: "How can I use what God has given me for earthly good and heavenly glory?"

Take your money and "make friends" by it. Build relationships by means of money so that when it's all said and done, the people you have helped may receive you into eternal dwellings.

It's amazing what you can do with a twenty-dollar bill. In many places of the world a prostitute would sell her body for it. You could get high from illegal drugs with it. You can get drunk from alcohol with it. You can go to the dollar store and buy twenty trinkets all made in China with it.

But you know what a Christian can do with it? He can use that twenty to pick up a homeless person and take him to Denny's and get him a Reuben sandwich, shake, and fries. And before the bill comes, he can start talking about spiritual things. Do you think the hitchhiker would listen? It's pretty likely.

How many Christians do you know who are looking for ways to be shrewd to share the gospel? Very few. We don't use our minds. We'll share a tract or invite someone to church, but if they don't come, we'll conclude that they are not of the elect. We just let it go. Jesus said to build relationships with your money.

Jesus admonishes us to be faithful in the little things because the little things determine whether you can handle the big things. When Jesus returns, where will you be in His kingdom? That depends. What have you done with the very little things? God gave you seventy or so years to live—what did you do with them? God gave you fifty or two hundred thousand dollars a year? What did you do with it? God gave you a spiritual gift. What did you do with it? Were you faithful in the very little things? Jesus asks, "Why should I entrust you with much?"

If I haven't used my money for eternal things, why should God come back and give me a high place to serve with Him? When the disciples asked how they would be rewarded for their sacrifices for Christ, He replied, "You also shall sit upon twelve thrones, judging the twelve tribes of Israel" (Matt. 19:28). They were faithful with the very little things.

Are Christians going to be judged one day? Yes, but not regarding salvation because Christ has made the sacrifice. Each one of us shall give an account of ourselves to God (Rom. 14:12)—were we faithful with the gifts and opportunities God gave us?

It is not what I did with my life. It is why I did it and for whom I did it. God calls me to be a steward of those things which He has given me. One day when we stand before God, our works shall be tested with fire to see which ones have eternal value (1 Cor. 3:11–15).

You and I will stand before God, and He will look at our lives. Did we live for Him or for ourselves? If we lived for ourselves, then God will blow it all away. I don't care how impressive it is right now—big houses, big cars, big reputations—it will be gone in the blink of an eye. He will look at the things we did for Him and reward us in eternity for those lasting works.

Some of the brightest lights in heaven will be the people you would never notice down here. God will say, "My child, you gave ten dollars a month to a missionary. Here is your valued place in the kingdom." Then He will look at someone like Corrie ten Boom who as a watchmaker's daughter didn't have two nickels to rub together, yet she devoted herself to eternal things all her life. It will be as Daniel prophesied, "Those who have insight will shine brightly like the brightness of the expanse of heaven, and those who lead the many to righteousness, like the stars forever and ever" (Dan. 12:3).

Your life is not an accident. The money, experiences, talents, and gifts you have received have been given to you for a purpose. You are a steward of these things for God. And I would be doing you a great injustice if I didn't tell you that He was going to call you to account.

Even though you may not hear it taught very often, the Scriptures are universal in reinforcing this truth. "All things are open and laid bare to the eyes of Him" (Heb. 4:13). "We must all appear before the judgment seat of Christ" (2 Cor. 5:10). We will reap what we sow, and "the one who sows to the Spirit will from the Spirit reap eternal life" (Gal. 6:8). We should know that "whatever good thing each one does, this he will receive back from the Lord" (Eph. 6:8). When the Philippians shared their resources with Paul, he could talk about the "profit which increases to [their] account" (Phil. 4:17). I could give you a dozen more Scriptures that all teach the same thing. Be shrewd in using your resources for the glory of God.

Money and a Successful Marriage

Money will be a big issue at some point in your marriage. It always is. I hear about it all the time from people who come to talk with me about their spouse. Let me give you some key biblical principles to help you circumvent some of these issues.

It's not my money; it's our money. In marriage, the two of you have become one flesh. Just because one person's name is on a paycheck doesn't mean they have anymore claim over that money. You both have equal say and can spend money however you want.

Out of courtesy, always check with your spouse before you make a major purchase. You don't want the bank or the credit card bill to surprise your spouse—it's much better to ask them beforehand. It shows honor and respect to your spouse to ask. It demonstrates that you are both in this thing together.

At the same time, both people need the freedom to do the things they need to do to keep the home running. A woman needs the freedom to run the home and spend money. A husband needs freedom to buy lawn mowers, tools, and so on. When husbands seek to control every purchase and decision, they are treating their wives like children. You will quickly lose the affection of your wife. Even when you have a budget, within that you have freedom to do what you need to do.

Decide who is going to keep the books in your family. The man doesn't always have to pay the bills and do the taxes. My wife does the books and does a wonderful job. The most important thing is that the person who has the responsibility needs to do it well. You can't mess up in the area of finances because there are too many consequences that will bring stress to your marriage.

Also, if your spouse is doing the books, submit to them and do the things necessary to help them be successful, like tracking purchases or saving receipts. Make it as easy as possible for them to succeed.

Recognize the differences between husband and wife. I'm lucky—my wife and I are basically the same type of spender when it comes to money. Often one spouse will be more conservative about spending, and the other will be a little bit looser. This can cause a lot of tension in your marriage. You need to discuss these differences and build flexibility into your marriage. Both of you will need to give a little bit out of love for your spouse. Don't try to dominate and change the other person. Meet in the middle and celebrate the spouse God has given you.

Corruption or Blessing?

The Bible says that corruption "is in the world by lust" (2 Pet. 1:4), and nowhere is this seen more clearly than with money. Money can be a source of tremendous blessing or enormous cursing. You will have to wrestle with temptation every day until your heart stops and your skin goes cold. God will judge what you have done with your resources. Pray and ask God to give you an eternal mind-set for how to use your money. You can't take it with you, but you can send it on ahead by finding biblical success.

How are you doing with the money God gave you? Are you wasting it, or are you enjoying it, using it, and investing it to the glory of God?

Biblical success comes when you

1. understand that God doesn't deal with everyone in the same way when it comes to money,
2. are humble concerning the resources you have been given,
3. learn not to depend on money for your future,
4. stay out of debt and live within your income,
5. learn how to use your money to enjoy life rather than endure it,
6. give your money to the church and use it for other good works,
7. store up eternal treasure by investing your money in Christ's work,

8. talk through the roles and responsibilities involved in using money within a marriage.

A Prayer for True Success

Father, You have blessed us with so much. Give us eyes to see Your sovereign hand in all we have. Help us know Your divine insight in how to use it. One day, allow us to feel Your majestic pleasure in judgment. Help us to use instead of hoard, to be stewards instead of owners, to bless and not just acquire. Let our money be a means of grace and not a nuisance and snare to true success in life. We ask this in Jesus' name. Amen.

Thinking More Deeply about True Success

1. What are the first one or two things you would do if you doubled your salary? Why?

2. Why is money such a source of temptation? How have you seen this in your own life or the lives of those around you?

3. Why is it so important to fix our hope on God if we are to have a right attitude about money? What steps can we take to ensure that we maintain this proper perspective?

4. Do you have trouble enjoying your money? Why or why not? How could change in this area help you find true success?

5. What are one or two of the most satisfying things you have ever done with your money? Why were these so meaningful to you?

Conclusion

Well, now that all has been said, I hope you have a more biblical and less twenty-first-century American view of success. Success is who you are, not what you collect.

Success is not merely that you succeed but what you succeed at. It is not that you achieved but what you achieved. It is that God is pleased with you, not that man is impressed by you. It is not about temporal happiness but lasting joy—that you have character to be respected, not mere popularity to be envied. This country has made a lifestyle of selling out to the former to achieve the latter.

One requires talent; the other, character and perseverance. One is of man; the other is of God. Human achievement fades quickly. True nobility is preserved in the memories of the next generations. It is called greatness. And when this is fleshed out in a human being in perfect flawlessness, it is the Person of Jesus Christ—God in the flesh. Our level of success will be exactly determined by how close we come to His likeness.

"The memory of the righteous is blessed" (Prov. 10:7).

Notes

Chapter 3

1. W. E. Sangster, *The Craft of Sermon Illustration* (London: Epworth Press, 1946).

Chapter 4

1. Paul Lee Tan, *Encyclopedia of 7,700 Illustrations* (Rockville, Maryland: Assurance Publishers, 1984).

2. T. L. Haines and L. W. Yaggy, *Royal Path of Life; or, Aims and Aids to Success and Happiness* (Nashville: Southwestern Publishing House, 1877).

Chapter 5

1. From Howard Walter's 1906 hymn "I Would Be True."

2. Donald Grey Barnhouse, *Let Me Illustrate* (Grand Rapids: Revell, 1994), 365–66.

Chapter 11

1. Peg Tyre et al., "The Power of No," *Newsweek* (September 13, 2004).

Chapter 12

1. Mark K. Matthews, "A Chosen Few," *Orlando Sentinel* (September 6, 2004): C.1.

Additional Resources from Tommy Nelson

*Ideal for Personal
or Group Bible Study*

Song of Solomon
Video Series (DVD or VHS)
Audio Series (CD)
112-page study guide

Song of Solomon for Students
Video Series (DVD or VHS)
Student study guide

A Life Well Lived
Video Series (DVD or VHS)
Audio Series (CD)
96-page study guide

The Big Picture:
Understanding the Story of the Bible
256-page soft-cover book that explains the
biblical narrative in an easy-to-read format

Live Conferences featuring Tommy Nelson
Hear Tommy speak live on *Song of Solomon* or *Ecclesiastes* in your area
at the Song of Solomon Conference or a Life Well Lived Conference.

**For more information call 800-729-0815
or visit www.TommyNelsonOnline.com**